Selected Poems *of* Georg Trakl

Translated by Bob Herz

Acknowledgements

Copyright © 2016 by Bob Herz

ISBN-10: 0-9976147-1-4
ISBN-13: 978-0-9976147-1-8

All rights reserved. No poem or artwork may be reproduced in full or in part without prior written permission from its owner.

Some of these poems have been previously published, or are forthcoming, in *Seneca review* and in *Nine Mile Magazine*.

First edition.

Nine Mile Press
4451 Cherry Valley Turnpike
LaFayette, NY 13084

Nine Mile Press is an imprint of Nine Mile Art Corp.

with love and more to Sally

Contents

Biographical Data	4
Introduction	7
Bibliography	35
I Aphorisms & Fragments	37
Aphorisms & Fragments	39
II The Breakthrough	43
Psalm (2nd Version)	45
Helian	47
III Sebastian in Dream	53
Section 1: Sebastian in Dream	55
Childhood	57
Song of Hours	58
On The Road	59
Landscape	61
To The Boy Elis	62
Elis	63
Hohenburg	65
Sebastian in Dream	66
On the Moor	69
In Spring	70
Evening in Lans	71
At the Mönchsberg	72
Kaspar Hauser Song	73
At Night	74
Metamorphosis of Evil	75
Section 2: Autumn of the Lonely	77
In the Park	79
A Winter Evening	80
The Cursed	81
Sonja	84
Along	85

Autumn Soul	86
Afra	87
Autumn of the Lonely	88
Section 3: Seven-song of Death	**89**
Rest & Silence	91
Anif	92
Birth	93
Decline	94
To One Who Died Young	95
Spiritual Twilight	96
Song of the West	97
Transfiguration	98
South Wind	99
The Wanderer	100
Karl Kraus	101
To the Silenced	102
Passion	103
Seven-song of Death	104
Winter Night	106
Section 4: Song of the Departed	**103**
In Venice	108
Limbo	109
The Sun	112
Song of a Captive Blackbird	113
Summer	114
End of Summer	115
Year	116
Occident	117
Springtime of the Soul	120
In Darkness	122
Song of the Departed	123
Section 5: Dream & Derangement	**125**
Dream & Derangement	127

IV	Published in *Der Brenner* 1914-5	133
	In Hellbrun	135
	The Heart	136
	Sleep	138
	Storm	139
	Evening	141
	Night	142
	Sadness	143
	Homecoming	144
	Lament	145
	Night Surrender	146
	In The East	147
	Klage	148
	Grodek	149
	Revelation & Decline	150

Biographical Data

1887   Trakl born in Salzburg, Austria. His father, Tobias, is a hardware dealer. The family is essentially middle-class. Trakl is the fifth of seven children.

1891   Trakl's sister Grete is born. She will be the subject of many of his poems. Some later critical studies suggest an incestuous relationship between the two. There is certainly an intensity between them, however characterized.

1897   Trakl enters the Salzburg Straatsgymnasium (Humanistic High School of the State). Prior to this he was enrolled in a Catholic school, though his religious training and upbringing were Protestant.

1901   He is forced to repeat fourth grade.

1904   First literary attempts. Becomes a member of "Apollo" (later "Minerva"), a Salzburg literary group which introduces him to the poetry of Baudelaire, Verlaine, & Hofmannsthal.

1905   Fails seventh grade and drops out of school to begin a three-year apprenticeship at a Salzburg pharmacy, the White Angel. First drug experiences. There are stories that by the end of his school years he carried a bottle of chloroform with him and dipped his cigarettes into an opium solution. The extreme mood swings that would characterize him for the remainder of his life begin at this time, and suicide threats become frequent.

1906   Writes two one-act plays, *All Souls' Day* and *Fata Morgana*. Both are failures, and he destroys all copies. His first literary work, a piece of impressionistic prose, is

	published in a local newspaper. He will publish a few more prose pieces in Salzburg newspapers, covering themes and settings found in his mature work
1908	First poem appears. Completes his pharmaceutical apprenticeship and enrolls in the University of Vienna for a two-year training course in pharmacy.
1909	Prepares a collection of poems, *Aus Goldenem Kelch* (*Out of a Golden Chalice*), but cannot find a publisher.
1910	Death of his father. Completes his iniversity courses and begins a one-year service in the Austro-Hungarian army, stationed with the medical corps in Vienna.
1911	Completes military services and returns to his pharmacy position at The White Angel. The job lasts two months. This is a period of increasing depressions and drug excesses.
1912	Returning to army service, he is assigned to a military hospital in Innsbruck. Becomes friends with Ludwig von Ficker, editor of *Der Brenner*, a literary journal in which he will publish poems regularly for the remaining two and a half years of his life. Nearly all of the poetry on which his reputation is based is written after he joins the *Der Brenner* circle. In this year also, he leaves active military service after a dispute with an officer. "Psalm" and "Helian," his artistic breakthroughs, are completed in this year and early 1913.
1913	Wanders in Vienna, Salzburg, and Innsbruck. Takes a job in the war ministry in Vienna, but quits in less than month. His first volume of poems, *Gedichte* (*Poems*) is published by Kurt Wolff, who also published Kafka's early writings. Gives his only public reading of his poems.

1914	A second volume of poems, S*ebastian im Traum* (*Sebastian in Dream*) is accepted for publication by Wolff. Through Ficker he receives an anonymous financial gift of 20,000 crowns from the philosopher Ludwig Wittgenstein. But with the outbreak of World War I he goes into active military service and never receives the money. He is sent as a lieutenant to the eastern front, where he cares for the wounded. He suffers frequent bouts of suicidal depression.
Later 1914	During the Battle of Grodek-Rawa Ruska of September 8-11, he is assigned sole care of 90 badly wounded soldiers sheltering in a barn, a task for which he is ill-prepared and lacks proper equipment. When one of the wounded ends his suffering by shooting himself in the head, Trakl flees outside only to be confronted by the sight of local peasants hanging lifeless in the trees. Later, during the retreat of the defeated Austro-Hungarian forces, he announces his intention to shoot himself, but is disarmed by his comrades. He suffers a nervous breakdown and spends a month in a hospital in Krakow. He sends a desperate note to Wittgenstein, who is also on the eastern front. Wittgenstein rushes to the hospital but arrives three days after Trakl has died of a self-inflicted overdose of cocaine.
1915	His final poems are printed in *Der Brenner*, and the book *Sebastian in Dream* appears from the Kurt Wolff publishing house. The book proves successful.

Introduction

1.

I felt that I knew the poetry of Georg Trakl before I ever read any of his poems. I was an undergraduate in the late '60's just learning my craft as a writer and discovering how much a poem could do. In that wonderful time it seemed possible to do everything and anything in poetry. The old rules had broken down, many seeming even precious. A poem by a poet I admired a great deal, James Wright, deeply impressed me. It was called "Rain":

> *It is the sinking of things.*
>
> *Flashlights drift over tall trees,*
> *Girls kneel,*
> *An owl's eyelids fall.*
>
> *The sad bones of my hands descend into a valley*
> *Of strange rocks.*

What was it about that poem? It seemed so slight, just 30 words, and yet—there was a density there that said everything it needed to say. It was about rain, but about so much more than rain. There was a snapshot of the whole world in there somehow, and a moment that encapsulated an eternity, transforming everything, including the speaker. I was astonished by the delicacy of the imagery, and by the way the imagery drove the narrative in what was really a plotless poem. I spent hours puzzling over how a line like "Girls kneel" could seem to have the same relative weight as "The sad bones of my hands descend into a valley," and how "Strange rocks" could seem the absolutely right conclusion to this poem. What are "strange rocks"? How could a phrase so close to being a cipher yet bring so much to the poem that it allowed a graceful and satisfying end? The images seem to have a mystical weight all their own, developed in or brought into the context of the poem. I loved how the poem seemed to imply something larger than itself, hinting at a view into another landscape, a place where we had never been but could almost see, because it was so familiar. I didn't understand it, and I wondered if maybe that sense of the larger unknown familiar world gave added meaning and weight to what was visible, those 30 words, bringing something just beyond definitional meanings to the individual words and phrases.

Reading these poems of James Wright, from the hugely influential books *The Branch Will Not Break* (1963) and *Shall We Gather At the River* (1967) I learned to read the poems of Georg Trakl, just as, perhaps, translating Georg Trakl, James Wright learned about a certain kind of magic he could bring to his poems, that would make them different from work he had done before, in *The Green Wall* (1957), which won the Yale Younger Poets Award, and *Saint Judas* (1959). He knew Trakl's poetry well. He had been translating and writing about it since his graduation from college in the 50's. The breakthrough came with the translations later gathered in the Sixties press book, *Twenty Poems of Georg Trakl*, with Robert Bly, which arguably started a revival of poetic and academic interest in Trakl's work and brought the poems to a larger public.

Wright was always honest about what he had learned from Trakl. He spoke about it in his 1975 *Paris Review* interview. It was the 1950's and he had just read a copy of Robert Bly's magazine *The Fifties*, which contained a poem by Trakl:

> *Some years earlier, at the University of Vienna, I had read in German the poetry of Trakl and I didn't know what to do with it, though I recognized that somehow it had a depth of life in it that I needed. Trakl is a poet who writes in parallelisms, only he leaves out the intermediary, rationalistic explanations of the relation between one image and another. I would suppose that Trakl has had as much influence on me as anybody else has had. But the interesting thing is that when I read Robert Bly's magazine, I wrote him a letter. It was sixteen pages long and single-spaced, and all he said in reply was, "Come on out to the farm." I made my way out to that farm, and almost as soon as we met each other we started to work on our translation of Trakl.*

I love the way Wright credits a poetic ancestor in this interview: *"I would suppose that Trakl has had as much influence on me as anybody else has had."* I don't mean to suggest, and I don't think he does here either, that there was imitation or borrowing involved between Wright and Trakl; there wasn't, at least not in any simple sense of adopting a voice or an imagery, or taking the pose of another. But there was influence. But Wright must have felt the power of the imagery and those a-rational methods of bringing the images into the field of the poem as he translated a piece like Trakl's "De Profundis":

>*It is a stubble field, where a black rain is falling.*
>*It is a brown tree, that stands alone.*
>*It is a hissing wind, that encircles empty houses.*
>*How melancholy the evening is.*
>
>*A while later,*
>*The soft orphan garners the sparse ears of corn.*
>*Her eyes graze, round and golden, in the twilight*
>*And her womb awaits the heavenly bridegroom.*
>
>*On the way home*
>*The shepherd found the sweet body*
>*Decayed in a bush of thorns.*
>
>*I am a shadow far from darkening villages.*
>*I drank the silence of God*
>*Out of the stream in the trees.*
>
>*Cold metal walks on my forehead.*
>*Spiders search for my heart.*
>*It is a light that goes out in my mouth.*
>
>*At night, I found myself on a pasture,*
>*Covered with rubbish and the dust of stars.*
>*In a hazel thicket*
>*Angels of crystal rang out once more.*

[Note that this version is from *Twenty Poems of Georg Trakl, Translated and Chosen by James Wright and Robert Bly* (Sixties Press, 1961). Some lines were altered when Wright later included the translation in *Above the River The Complete Poems*, James Wright (Farrar, Straus and Giroux; Reprint edition April, 1992)].

You can see the delicacy of imagery and the "leaving out the intermediary" development of it in many of the poems in that original Twenty Poems book. Take a poem like "Sleep"

> *Not your dark poisons again,*
> *White sleep!*
> *This fantastically strange garden*
> *Of trees in deepening twilight*
> *Fills up with serpents, nightmoths,*
> *Spiders, bats.*
> *Approaching stranger!*
> *Your abandoned shadow*
> *In the red of evening*
> *Is a dark pirate ship*
> *Of the salty oceans of confusion.*
> *White birds from the outskirts of the night*
> *Flutter out over the shuddering cities*
> *Of steel.*

It is not just the method of setting images forth without narrative connectives, and letting them speak for themselves, so that the images become the narrative, that Wright learned from his work with Trakl, and put to such impressive and profound use in his own poems. You can also feel in these poems—in Wright's "Rain" and Trakl's "De Profundis" and "Sleep"—that sense of a larger world hinted at and viewed through a smaller space. Wright felt this powerful force just as others have felt it. Rilke felt it and described it this way: *"I imagine that even those standing close shall still experience these views and insights as if through a window-pane: since Trakls' experience goes as if in reflections and fills his whole room, which is unenterable, like the room in a mirror. (Who could he have been?)"* I like this comment a lot, with that description of a wide vista in enclosed space circling back endlessly on itself. The philosopher Martin Heidegger has also made some penetrating comments on the poems, in the way they open and close, present and distance themselves and their objects and images in what he describes as the four-fold nature of reality (earth and sky, divinities and mortals). It is the way that Heidegger apprehends the nearness and distance of poetry —Trakl's poetry, but also by extension all poetry—that struck me as revealing something about the nature of this poetry that is also apparent in the passage quoted above from Rilke. I also like this by Robert Bly: *"The poems of Georg Trakl have a magnificent silence in them. It is very rare that he himself talks—for the most part he allows the images to speak for him."* The images speak, not the poet. It is a brilliant comment, and perfectly describes the feeling we get reading the poems.

2.

I love this poetry. There is nothing else like it in my reading experience, in the choices of imagery, the construction of the poems, the essential *otherness* of the work. The closest I have seen are perhaps Rilke's *Sonnets to Orpheus*, which also occupy this strange ground of implication, multiple meaning, and ambiguity, with rapid leaps from image to image and sudden changes in diction and tone, and a somehow coherent narrative plotlessness. I have tried to translate these poems in ways that make them more accessible without sacrificing that essential strangeness.

I should perhaps also note here that translating poetry from the German is an interesting and sometimes frustrating exercise, as sentence structure and use of verb tenses is much different in German than English. Mark Twain has a famous example: *"But when he, upon the street, the (in-satin-and-silk-covered-now-very-unconstrained-after-the-newest-fashioned-dressed) government counselor's wife met."* Funny, but alas, also accurate. This is all made more difficult in poetry, especially Trakl's poetry, which bends grammar to somewhere near its breaking point and pushes ambiguity often far beyond its breaking point. Others have written, for example, about the difficulty of bringing Trakl's neologisms and compound words into English, or of getting the right meaning of the several connotations of a word like "wild" which is used in reference to non-domestic animals. The word is generally understood as a hunting term, close to our word "game," though neither that word or the often rendered "deer" carries quite the same weight. Some have suggested "prey" as a possibility, although that brings another set of connotations to English readers. In these translatuions, I have tried to render it in ways that are sensitive to context. One more example of this ambiguity in words used and chosen: the German word "Geschlecht" can mean "sex," "race," "family," or "generation." This is significant for a line in the poem "Helian": *Erschütternd ist der Untergang des Geschlechts* which I render, "The ruin of a generation is shattering," but which could also mean and entail all of the other word possibilities.

It is probably best to simply acknowledge that every translation is also an act of homage, and another version of an untouched original. These are my versions, and I know that there will be plenty of opportunity for readers to quibble with my word choices, sentence structure, and referents in this volume. Others have chosen different words or sometimes have published different understandings of lines or phrases. Their translations are wonderful and I am indebted to all of them. I learned something reading them, found something new and often wonderful in the words, or the lines, or the translated poems as a whole. I hope this work will add something also.

3.

I want to talk about Trakl's life here, before discussing some of the poems. I include a brief outline of the key events in Trakl's life in the Biographical Data section of this book. I do not think it was a happy life. He seems from his letters to have lived in an almost constant state of suffering and depression. He was frequently broke, probably in part because of the expense of his multiple addictions to drugs and alcohol. Poetry seems to have been the stable center of his life after his teen years. He worked constantly on his poetry, wherever he was, revising carefully —even in the hospital after his breakdown and a few days before his suicide, he gave his friend Ficker his two final poems (the masterpieces "Klage" and "Grodek"), and revisions of several others. He wanted them to be right, to accurately reflect his vision. There was nothing spontaneous or thrown off about them.

What was he like? We don't know much about him in any personal way. There are not enough letters, or enough in the letters, to provide a full personal portrait. We know that he had a powerful physical presence, and that his friends were more or less awed by him. He was blonde, muscular, above middle height. His eyes are interesting, in the pictures they appear somewhat closed, as if looking somewhere farther away, through us, perhaps, or past us.

Here is an account by his dedicated friend and supporter, Ludwig von Ficker, describing his first meeting with Trakl at the Café Maximilian in Innsbruck. This was on May 22, 1912, two years before the poet's death. Ficker was editor of the literary magazine *Der Brenner*, around which a group of artists and poets had formed:

> *Once again I arrived there soon after noon in order to meet at the so-called Brenner table of friends. I had hardly sat down, however, when at some distance a man stood out, who sat between two windows, which looked out over Maria Theresia Street, on a plush sofa and with open eyes seemed to ponder before himself. His hair was cut short, with a tinge of silver, the face of indeterminable age: oh, thus the stranger sat there, in an attitude, which was instinctively attractive and nevertheless betrayed an aloofness. But I already noticed, he also saw, apparently turned inward, with searching gaze repeatedly over toward us, and, hardly had I appeared, it did not last very long before a waiter handed his card to me: Georg Trakl. I stood up pleased—because shortly before I had published his poem "Surburb in Foehn"—, welcomed him and asked him to our table.*

Interesting, no? He was aloof, pondering himself, quiet yet standing out, a man with a face of indeterminate age, instinctively attractive, but interested enough in the world around him and perhaps ambitious enough to send over his card. It was a fortunate meeting. Ficker became his champion and published many of his poems in *Der Brenner*.

We know that Trakl was brought up in a middle class household, with servants and a sense of the importance of culture. His father had a successful hardware business in Salzburg, his mother was a reserved woman who suffered bouts of extreme depression for which she took opium and then retired in her room for days at a time. Georg was the fourth of her six children who survived to adulthood. There was some problem in the house, however, between Georg and his mother. As he grew older, he became hostile not only to the experience of the bourgeoisie class that he was born into, but especially hostile toward her. We can see this hostility in the imagery of some of the poems, for example in the powerful opening lines to "Sebastian in Dream":

> *Mother carried the infant in the white moon,*
> *In the shade of the walnut tree, the ancient elder,*
> *Drunk with the sap of the poppy...*

The family member closest to him was his sister Grete. She was five years younger than him, and looked like him. Like his, her life was short and characterized in emotional instability and drug dependency, and ended like his in suicide in 1917, when she shot herself at a party. Her image recurs almost obsessively in his poems, and seems to some to suggest an incestuous relationship:

> *The strange sister appears again in someone's evil*
> * dream.*
> *Resting in the hazel-bush she toys with his stars.*
> *The student, or perhaps his double, gazes after her a*
> * long time from the window.*

He did not do well in the authoritarian schools that prevailed in Germany at the time. He was not a good student. In his fourth year he failed Latin, Greek, and mathematics, and had to repeat the work; in his seventh year he failed these same subjects again, and dropped out of school altogether. His response to the school culture that he hated so much was personal and antagonistic, as he adopted increasingly eccentric dress and behavior. Introduced to narcotics by one of his classmates, a pharmacist's son, by the end of his school career he was carrying around a little bottle of chloroform and dipping his cigarettes into an opium solution.

He joined a writer's club in 1904, "Apollo" (later "Minerva"). They met in cafes and read poems to each other, cultivating the latest avant-garde fashion, and asserting their independence from the bourgeoisie. The group did not produce much good work, but through it and others like it, Trakl was exposed to authors who would influence him in his writing career—Neitzche, Baudelaire, Verlaine, and others.

In 1905 he made a decisive career move, being hired as an apprentice in a Salzburg pharmacy, the White Angel. From here, after a three-year apprenticeship, he would be eligible for a two year course at the University of Vienna, after which he could be licensed as a pharmacist. But selecting a career was only a partial surrender to the necessities of earning money to live and eat, for he also became even more bohemian at this time, wearing his hair long, dressing like a dandy, and making it clear to anyone who would listen that he was opposed to middle class mores and life. Perhaps this was his response to even having to make such choices, an assertion of his freedom against life's necessities. In one more demonstration of anti-bourgeoisie behavior, he discovered brothels at this time, and would sit in them for hours, drinking wine, playing the part of revolutionary or *poete maudit*, as he delivered anti-bourgeoisie rants to the female prostitutes.

His manic-depressive symptoms began to appear at this time also—moments of joy followed by depression and silence, even thoughts of suicide. He spoke about how real these things were and how much they affected him in a 1908 letter to his older sister Minna: *"I have experienced, smelled, touched, the most frightening possibilities within myself, have heard the demons howling in my blood, the thousand devices with their spurs which drive the flesh mad."* This is a horrifying vision, but it was followed by an experience in which he says he has become *"all living ear, again listen[ing] to the melodies inside me, and my winged eye again dreams its images, which are more beautiful than all reality."* [This letter quoted from Lindenberger, *Trakl*].

He was never able to get these wild mood swings under control, but in his poetry he learned to exemplify them. The poems became narratives of images moving quickly from joy to sorrow, idyll to fallen world, much as he experienced the world and his symptoms himself. Indeed, if there is an easily visible personal aspect to these poems, it is in the way the poems replicate his changes of outlook and mood. These changes were not imagined, they were what he lived with: They were his life, and they became the substance and construct of his greatest poems.

Trakl's father died in 1910, and although his mother ran the business for awhile, profits fell, and he could no longer count on receiving enough money to pay for his increasingly expensive alcohol and drug habits. He entered the army for a one year tour of duty, a decision that some have suggested may have been a way of delaying decisions about what to do with his life. When his service ended, he still had made no decisions about a career. He seems not to have been suited for much. He had his pharmaceutical education, of course, and took a job on a pharmacy, but found the work emotionally draining, especially the parts that involved waiting on customers. He lasted less than two months on that job, and then re-enlisted in the army, where he was assigned to a post in the pharmacy of the army hospital at Innsbruck.

This was also the time when he became a member of the intellectual circle of writers and philosophers clustered around the semimonthly journal *Der Brenner*. These artists saw themselves as fighting for the integrity of art against the urban decadence of their colleagues in the big cosmopolitan city of Vienna. Their support, and the exposure he gained by being published in the magazine, made a significant difference in the confidence he had in his writing and in his ambitions for his poetry. His great poems date from this time, and from late 1912 until his death in 1914, every issue of the journal had at least one Trakl poem.

He came under another important influence at about this time. In 1912, Trakl read the poetry of Arthur Rimbaud in a German translation. The exposure was significant. Under Rimbaud's influence, his poems changed from rhymed to free verse, and became more complex.

Breakthroughs came in the poems "Psalm," and "Helian." The power of these new poems was evident: "Helian" was hailed almost immediately as a major work. His first book, *Poems*, was published in 1912, by the same publisher who had published Kafka. He was writing well, he was published, he was being noticed. But though there seemed to be many good things happening with his poetry, his difficulties in finding a job and making a living continued. He was hired by the labor department in Vienna, but quit after two hours. He went to work in 1913 at the war ministry in Vienna, but quit after less than a month. As he began to prepare a second volume of poems, *Sebastian im Traum*, he received a large and what should have been a stabilizing gift from an anonymous donor, who turned out to be Ludwig Wittgenstein. This was in July 1914. Wittgenstein had decided to give away his inheritance to worthy artists and poets. Unfortunately, Trakl was called back into active service for World War I before he could receive the gift.

He was not happy. A note he gave Ficker at about this time showed his feelings: *"The feeling at those times closest to death: that all are worthy of love. Then waking to the world bitterness; your sin remains; your poem an imperfect atonement."* He was entering a depressive phase, filled with guilt for unspecified offenses, finding a necessary but insufficient expiation in his poems. Clearly something was amiss.

Things got worse when he returned to the front. After the Battle of Grodek, he was assigned the care of 90 badly wounded men, a task for which he lacked adequate training or equipment. It must have been nightmarish duty. He heard a shot, and learned that one of the men in his care had shot himself. He hurried to the bedside to find parts of the man's brain still sticking to the wall. Unable to bear the sight, he rushed outside, only to be confronted by a further nightmare: There were corpses hanging from the trees. These were members of the local population whom Austrian authorities suspected of disloyalty. The terrible pressure this created on Trakl's already depressed psyche must have been unbearable. At dinner with his fellow officers he declared that he could no longer go on, and he rushed outside to try to shoot himself. Fortunately, his companions disarmed him, and sent him to the hospital for treatmnt.

Ficker visited him there and heard him read his two final poems, "Klage" and "Grodek," masterpieces written at the front. At Ficker's urging he also wrote to Wittgenstein, whom he had never met, to ask him to visit. Wittgenstein was serving on the eastern front, and though he made the effirt, it took time for him to reach the hospital. Unfortunately, within the week, Trakl took an overdose of the cocaine that he had managed to keep hidden from hospital authorities. He remained in coma for a day, dying on November 3. He was 27 years old. By the time Wittgenstein reached him, he had been dead for three days. He was buried in Krakow. He was celebrated almost immediately as a major poet.

4.

Heidegger has a beautiful essay—really a lecture—on Trakl and language in which he talks about the naming and calling functions of the poetry, by which he means that we hear the naming and calling of the poem in our physical space, but the poetry brings the things named and called no nearer to us. What comes near to us is the presence of things in language, a "presence sheltered in absence." We have this sense of continuously when reading Trakl, that things have been summoned, that we can feel their presence here very powerfully, and yet—they are not here. Heidegger says, *"The things that were named, thus called, gather to themselves sky and earth, mortals and divinities,"* a remark almost as mystical as some of those in Trakl's poems.

In the structure of this book, along with translations of all the late poems I've included some short pieces and fragments, which may be useful to the reader for what they reveal about the poet, and two poems in which I think Trakl broke through, and found his true voice. The remainder of this section deals selectively with some of the poems in the book. My comments on these poems are not, and are not intended to be, exhaustive; rather they show ways of reading the poems which were helpful to me and which I hope may be useful to others.

But before turning to specific poems, I want to mention a couple of things about technique, the method of composition, the use of imagery, and the motive force in many of the poems.

It is important to know that Trakl was a careful and constant reviser of his work. Nothing appears in his poems accidentally. It is all meant to be where it is. Walther Killy has a wonderful piece (in his *Über Georg Trakl*, Göttingen, Vandenhoeck & Ruprecht, 1967; quoted in *Song of the West*, North Point Press, 1988, tr Robert Firmage). Killy talks about the phrase: "...a smile full of sorrow and humility..." found in the notes for the poem "Winter Night." Trakl's notes show that it started out as a "smile full of sorrow and arrogance."

> *Then he replaced "arrogance" immediately with its opposite, "humility," considered anew, restored "arrogance" again, crossed it out once more, and in its place put "shame." This word he also exchanged for its opposite, and from it made "a smile full of sorrow and pride." Finally he returned in the manuscript to the expression "sorrow and humility," which was transformed once more, in a final decision over the galley proofs, to "arrogance," the definitive version.*

Here is the section in my translation:

Bitter snow & moon!
A red wolf strangled by an angel. Your legs rattle as you walk like blue ice & a smile of sadness & arrogance turns your face to stone & your forehead grows pale with the lust of frost;
or it leans silently over the sleep of a watchman, sunk in his wooden hut.

Was this a difficult word choice, "arrogance" or "humility" or "shame" or whatever? Clearly it was for him. He had to think his way through the images to get to the final selection. Read in context is seems plain that only "arrogance" would work in the line. But it is interesting that he wasn't choosing among small gradients of words and meanings. There is a tremendous distance between the words arrogance and humility. I think he was testing something, the limits of the meaning here, the limits of his vision—or maybe the truth of that vision. He wasn't inventing, he was transcribing something seen: It was reality. He had to make it right, precise, true. Considering the instability of his life and his addictions, his failed careers, and the evidence we have seen that poetry was his stabilizing center, it may not be over-dramatic to suggest that he chose and revised his words and poems as if his life depended on it.

I talked above about the sense of the broader world that Trakl's poems imply. One way he achieves this effect is by his use of language, the joining of unexpected words, the presentation of unexpected actions and actors. In the "Winter Night" poem, there is the "red wolf strangled by an angel," a striking image whose reality could hold us in contemplation for a long time, but not something of this quotidian world. In "South Wind" he speaks of "Blind cries of the wind, moonlike days of winter," wonderful choices of words that convey a reality, and then of "Childhood, steps softly fading near black hedge…" which for me can summon up an entire period in the youth of a person's life. I find all of these images wholly unexpected and wonderful. They are stated with such confidence and precision that we as readers are called to affirm them as real, not perhaps real for us, but real somewhere, in that implied reality that the poems seem to suggest, and that we assent to on entering them.

I think that much of Trakl's poetry springs from a motive having to do with his sense of guilt, shown in that note he gave to Ficker at the time of his last mobilization: *The feeling at those times closest to death: that all are worthy of love. Then waking to the world bitterness; your sin remains; your poem an imperfect atonement.* Here is much of the reason he is driven to write: It is against his sense a non-specific, unnamed, and perhaps unnamable sin, and his statement that writing is thus an "imperfect atonement." For Trakl, writing was redemption, it was the way he saved his life, how he demonstrated that he was capable of salvation. The writing became, I suspect, in its imperfection as atonement, an act that had to be repeated, that he did not dare to stop.

The Fragments

Much as I love the completed poems, there is something about fragments that always seems so very revealing. They seem unguarded, like casual remarks that suddenly shine a light on character. We've all had the experience—a friend's joke over beer that reveals an unexpected lost love, a snide whispered remark that exposes something unexpectedly venal and small, the arbitrary line-drawing of a colleague in the middle of a too-long meeting that shows the gateway to the heart.

Consider for our purposes a phrase from the fragments like "It is God's peace. The evening shadows linger." Lovely. Also mysterious. You could puzzle over this for a long time. Is it aspirational? Maybe. It is certainly a showing from the Edenic part of the poet's psyche, but it is a moment that is quickly followed by signs from the other manic, demonic, opposing side, in this case the blackbird singing in the autumn trees that begins the third stanza. In another fragment we read: "When I collapsed on the black hill of Sleep / weary of the wild land & the desperation of bleak winterdays, / the vision came to me suddenly on glowing wing..." We have here desperate winter collapse and an unstated vision in a wild land—but importantly, vision is what is conferred here, in this desolation, at the terrible pitch of collapse. In another fragment, we get this: "Munch woke at the edge of the wood toward evening. A gold cloud faded above him & the dark peace of autumn filled him with fear." Now the Edenic has become a place of fear, not of salvation or rest. These are not complete poems, but they are glimpses into the tortured vision that produces the other works.

First Breakthrough: "Psalm"

There are two poems that I believe show the moment when Trakl finds his true voice. It is incredibly exciting—so exciting that even now, reading them, you can feel that onrush of energy as the discovery of true voice is being made. The first is "Psalm," written in 1912. The second is "Helian," discussed below.

"Psalm" is an unrhymed poem—his first successful usage—and longer than any of his earlier poems, with a new tone and new ambition. It is visionary and inclusive, an opening of the field, to borrow a phrase from Robert Duncan. From here on his work becomes more visionary and other-directed, both more comprehensive and also more mysterious. It becomes recognizably the mature poetry of this extraordinary poet.

Several things in this poem are different than his earlier work. The long lines, for instance, which you can feel are necessary to the poem's development and the credibility of the images. The catalogue and the hnts of story, of narratuve. The use of parallel syntax and sentence structures is also new (the "There is…" parallel structure and the extended use of simple declarative sentences depicting actions in ways that come to seem parallel, so that all seem to acquire an equal weight. I would argue that this parallel syntax is its metric). Others may have helped him find and develop this structure. He may have seen something similar in poems by Whitman and Rimbaud. This sense of influence was noted by Lindenberger in his book on Trakl, and I am grateful for the insight.

One of the poems he notes as a possible influence is Section 15 of *Song of Myself*:

15

The pure contralto sings in the organ loft,
The carpenter dresses his plank, the tongue of his foreplane
   whistles its wild ascending lisp,
The married and unmarried children ride home to their
   Thanksgiving dinner,
The pilot seizes the king-pin, he heaves down with a strong arm,
The mate stands braced in the whale-boat, lance and harpoon
   are ready,
The duck-shooter walks by silent and cautious stretches,
The deacons are ordain'd with cross'd hands at the altar,
The spinning-girl retreats and advances to the hum of the big
   wheel,
The farmer stops by the bars as he walks on a First-day loafe
   and looks at the oats and rye,
The lunatic is carried at last to the asylum a confirm'd case….

And there is the Rimbaud, perhaps sections III and IV from the poem "Childhood" in *Illuminations*:

III

In the woods there is a bird; his song stops you and makes you
   blush.

There is a clock that never strikes.
There is a hollow with a nest of white beasts.
There is a cathedral that goes down and a lake that goes up.
There is a little carriage abandoned in the copse or that goes
  running down the road beribboned.
There is a troupe of little actors in costume, glimpsed on the
  road through the border of the woods.
And then, when you are hungry and thirsty, there is someone
  who drives you away.

IV

I am the saint at prayer on the terrace like the peaceful beasts
  that graze down to the sea of Palestine.
I am the scholar of the dark armchair. Branches and rain
  hurl themselves at the windows of my library.
I am the pedestrian of the highroad by way of the dwarf
  woods; the roar of the sluices drowns my steps. I can see
  for a long time the melancholy wash of the setting sun....

But these are influences, not the core of the poem, not its subject or its vision. They are the ladders, if you will, that Trakl had to climb to find his voice somewhere in that second or third story of the house of poetry, and that he then left behind. He modified whatever he saw, and fitted it to his own usage. To say that he saw such techniques elsewhere does not detract from the originality or the scope of his achievement here. (It is interesting to note that he did not use these long lines again, which may have been a possible way of distancing himself from this debt.)

Several actions and images in "Psalm" are mysterious and fragmentary. I think the poem earns all of its mystery. Think of those actions that seem barely defined yet important to the narrative of the poem ("They bury the Stranger." "The dead orphans lay on the garden wall." There are tales of the South Seas and exotic or erotic dances but also of the scorched orchard: the idyll cohabits a space with the desolate, the Garden with the wasteland that has followed this Apocalypse of the lost Paradise, and the dead and dying and the filth-stained Angels. This is not a standard narrative structure; it is rather, I believe, a way of making an argument, and of describing a world. There is a story being told, and we glimpse it, but never see it full; because the story *is* the argument.

And then there is that final line, so astounding in the way it brings in the extra-sensual level of reality: God watches all. This is the needed final statement to the argument. We feel its necessity as we read it, its weight, its power: We feel that its placement is exactly where it needs to be. The statement is not a judgment on what has gone before it in the poem, not an inversion as in, say, a sonnet's end-lines, or a poetic conclusion in any ordinary sense, but rather the opening of a door to another consideration, an invitation to look again and feel again all that we have witnessed in the poem. This God is not an actor. He is silent in his gazing, more a deist God than the intervenor God of Christianity. He sees what is here, but does not act upon it, does not speak, does not judge. He only watches over Golgotha as the poet describes this doomed world in tones that seem totally objective, factual, without intrusion or judgment by the poet.

His eyes are gold: Gold!

Second Breakthrough: "Helian"

The other great breakthrough poem is "Helian." Trakl called the poem "the most precious and painful I have ever written." He wrote it between December 1912 and January 1913. I believe that the poem earned his description by dealing in new ways with related themes that were difficult for him, as they would be for anyone: the decline of family, and of civilization, and the various fragmented forms of an individual character making its way in this disintegrating and disorienting world.

As in "Psalm," the poem hints throughout at a broader narrative or broader themes that are not revealed or fully described, and it does so in a compelling train of obsessive images, some angelic, some chthonic, both sides necessary to the structure. The powerful imagery makes the poem easy to read, and the several burdens it bears make it harder to analyze; it is clear at the level of those images, but difficult at the level of what we might call classical critical discourse. The heart understands, as does the spirit; but the mind struggles. As I say, it could not have been an easy poem to write.

In order to make this poem, Trakl developed a new form for his writing, going even beyond the innovations of "Psalm." In this new form, there is no plot as such, but there is a narrative which is entirely composed at the level of the images. He addresses his broad themes of the decline of western civilization in a rich series of images that convey the ironic beauty of that disintegration, and parallel to it, he describes a family's loss, as disease and spiritual prostitution, and the ultimate ruin of death.

The theme of the decline of western civilization shows in such lines as "The ruin of a generation is shattering" or "Evening, & the bells that no longer ring sink down, / The black walls on the town-square fall to ruin, / The dead soldier is calling to a prayer." And the generational loss of family as a unit and spiritual force shows in lines like: "A pale angel, / The son enters the empty house of his fathers. // The sisters have gone far away to white old men." And throughout there is the Christian archetypal imagery of death and resurrection, shown in the way Helian survives bodily decay and leprosy to resurrect at the end of the poem, when "The silent god lowers his blue lids over him."

I also see something personal in the poem, though this may be an idiosyncratic reading on my part. It is what I mentioned above, the way the poem catches the movement of the poet's mind, in the rapid imagistic movement in the poem from Garden to Wasteland, from "The peach has a red glow in the leaves" to the "branches that are rotting, along walls full of leprosy," and in the depiction of the several fragmented guises of the protagonist.

Trakl talks about this psychic movement and the nature of self in the 1908 letter to his older sister Minna that I cited above: *"I have experienced, smelled, touched, the most frightening possibilities within myself, have heard the demons howling in my blood, the thousand devices with their spurs which drive the flesh mad,"* and that subsequent state in which he says he has become *"all living ear, again listen[ing] to the melodies inside me, and my winged eye again dreams its images, which are more beautiful than all reality."*

Were see that same extreme alternation between the demonic and the angelic throughout this poem, and as a characteristic in the poems that follow. I suggest that the exchange between the two enacts on the page an emotional picture of the movement of the poet's mind, and it creates the dynamic structure for these poems.

In this poem we also see the protagonist appear in several forms—walking in the sun in the lonely hours of the spirit, the youth who enters the house, and the stranger, the young novice, the mad boy, the "soul [that] looks at itself in the rosy mirror," and the other figures. The personality presented does not grow or progress; rather it is discontinuous, shifting, and perhaps, if all these forms are taken together, comprehensive; it is, in this reading, a hall of mirrors that through all its many distortions can finally and truly reflect a single person. This discontinuous character of the protagonist and of other figures will also appear in other subsequent poems. It is more than method; it is part of the information of the poems. We see something similar regarding narrators and forms of more or less plotless narration in other post-Romantic poems that appeared within a decade or so of "Helian": in T.S. Elliot's "The Wasteland," or in sections of Ezra Pound's "The Cantos." These poems are not lyrics, or Romantic poems in the old style; there is no overt personal reference or expression of the writer's experience. A new thing is being birthed in these lines, this structure. Nothing like it had existed before. Trakl brought poetry to a new place with this major poem.

The Elis Poems

The two Elis poems, "To The Boy Elis" and "Elis," were written between spring, 1913, and early 1914, part of the same flowering that began with "Helian" and "Psalm." The poems began as a single poem, until Trakl saw that the sections were pulling apart, and separated them. The Elis figure is literary, taken from E. T. A. Hoffmann's tale, "The Mines at Falun." In that story the character Elis Frobom is a 17th century Swedish miner who dies in the mines on his wedding day. His body is recovered 50 years later, and is still youthful, perfectly preserved by the airless mine shaft. Seeing the corpse, his now-aged wife embraces him, and his body crumbles to dust. The story sets up a series of oppositions about youth and age, innocence and experience, and the passing of time.

In the first Elis poem, "To the Boy Elis," we see striking imagery that is part of the so-called "blue world" that filled many of Trakl's late poems. These blue world images are related figures and objects drawn from opposing categories of pastoral idyl and demonic disintegration. The idyll images appear as wood, spring, the gentle animal, the blackbird, the grapes, the blueness, and the demonic appear in the images of the black cave, the black dew, the bleeding forehead, the ruined stars, the attempted prophetic interpretation of the bird's flight, the monk who dips his fingers into the flowering of the dead body. The sounding of the thorn-bush echoes the burning bush from which God spoke to Moses. The world, or worlds, conjured by this long-dead Elis are so fragile that at last even the stars are ruined and can only share their final gold.

This blue world imagery seems to be an influence from the blue flower imagery of the German poet, author, and philosopher Novalis, (Georg Philipp Friedrich Freiherr von Hardenberg, May 2, 1772 – March 25, 1801), an early German Romantic. The blue flower appears in Novalis' novel *Heinrich von Ofterdingen*. In the book the young Heinrich rejects bourgeois materialism to search for artistic and spiritual fulfillment, symbolized by a perfect blue flower. He says, "It is not treasures that I care for, but I long to see the blue flower. I cannot rid my thoughts of the idea, it haunts me." The image was very powerful and became a symbol of the German Romantic movement.

Trakl certainly knew about the blue flower, and about Novalis. He dedicated one of his poems to Novalis, and in an early draft of the poem he mentioned the blue flower. But this is an influence, not a conquest; Trakl's adoption of the blue imagery is not slavish, and the images and landscapes he describes in these final poems are variable, even one might say provisional. It is, for example, a dual symbol, invoking the color of the world before dawn as well as at evening; in other words, it is the blue of beginnings and endings.

The narrative of this poem moves from life to death: from "you move your arms more beautifully in the blue" to "How long, Elis, you have been dead," from grapes to black dew, from the thorn-bush with its suggestions of the divine to the animal that lowers its heavy lids, from the call of the blackbird to the ruined stars. It is a narrative told in images not actions, a gradual passing of life and innocence to death and ruin.

It is easy to get carried away by the beauty of the images of this first Elis poem and lose the narrative thread that carries us along to the loss of life and beauty. Not so with the second Elis poem, which ends in nothingness, the wind's lonely desolation. As in the first Elis poem, this one includes a direct address, speaking to an Elis who appears in perfect repose in the perfect stillness of a golden day. But unlike "To The Boy Elis," this poem brings with it a different and more expansive range of associations. Many of these have been the subject of intense and often interesting critical labor. For example, the images of the fisherman and the shepherd are said to be drawn from the Gospel of John, the moon as a golden boat in the sky is from Neitzche's *Also Sprak Zarathustra*, the image of Elis sinking his head on the black cushion is from Hoffman's "Mines of Falun," and the old man's song from Hofmannsthal's version of the same tale, the icy sweat and God's wind from a German translation of Rimbaud, and the whole image structure with its opposed visions of life is from a poem by Holderlin, "Halfte des Lebens" ("Middle of Life").

This is wonderful critical work, though it doesn't do much to explain the mysterious power of the poem for readers unaware of these sources. My own sense is that the power of the poem has to do with its grasp and description of archetypal images and transitions, things that move us whether we are consciously aware of them or not. The poem opens in an Eden, a place of perfect silence and perfect days, and slowly, over its twenty-nine lines, moves us to the loss of innocence and the final vision of desolation—God's lonely wind sounding endlessly on black walls.

When we first meet Elis he is a figure of love, a Cupid with blue eyes that mirror the sleep of lovers and a mouth where rosy love-sighs are silenced by (I assume) their kisses. In the righteousness of his days he sees the fisherman pull in his nets and the shepherd lead his herd along the forest's edge. Beautiful pastoral images. But then night comes, ending the perfect day, and Elis' heart trembles in a lonely heaven. The world was beautiful, but now Elis is separated from it, a dweller in a lonely heaven, not part of this idyll anymore. Innocence and beauty and perfection are lost. He has moved to the other world, and it is lonely there.

The second part of the poem describes this loneliness and loss: his head sinking on black cushions, the blue deer that is bleeding, the brown tree that is dead, the night pond that absorbs the stars and signs, and suddenly the new season of winter come behind the hill. The world is turned not to the demonic but to death, the absence of life. The final image is of the wind from God sounding over a lifeless place, "along black walls." It is a thoroughly beautiful and completely depressing poem.

My sense is that in these archetypes and images, the poem continues to open out, to expand its range of—"meanings" is too strong a word—its allusions. The poem opens itself to other interpretations in this sequence of words and images: for example, the poem could be read to be about aging, about the process of moving from the world of innocence and youth to age and death, the loss of the ripe world to the world of winter and decomposition. Whatever it suggests, and however you read it, it is an extremely powerful poem, whose meanings continue to broaden long after the reading is done.

Storm

"Storm" is one of the half-dozen or so poems Trakl completed in the months before his suicide in 1914. It maintains the technique of narrative construction the great poems "Helian" and "Elis" as a form of symbolic argument, but much else is new. There is, for example, the use of plural nouns—mountains, fathers, mothers, eagles, spirits, etc.—as if to describe an entire world by classes and categories, and the inescapable sense of violence or potential violence that seems to occupy this world. We don't learn much about the speaker. He speaks directly to mountains, eagles, flowers, silence, and other things, and describes the elements and metamorphoses of this world; but he does not speak to us or talk about himself to us. We overhear him describe his fear as a snake and tell it to die, and describe his tears, and his works, and the purifying fire in the short breathless phrases of hysteria, in the confusion of lines and images of someone overwhelmed by emotions. We move rapidly from calmness to rage to fear and anger, each emotional state metamorphosing into the next, each attended and described by a sequence of external and internal images.

We notice how the poem moves from mountains to silence to final fire; and from the gold clouds of the first stanza, the fear and terror of family in the second, to the burning sorrow of the God of the third stanza, and then to the purifying fire of the final lines. Or the way the mountains that are the "noble / Grief of eagles" become the setting for menacing thunder and wild streams of tears. By these means, the poem is telling us that something has taken place during its course that rends the night and is purified by fire. The poem does not go so far as to say that it must be purified that way, only that it is; yet I find it hard to read those last lines as other than the fatal necessary conclusion of the story being told.

For there is a story, or at least, the hint of one that comes, as in so many of Trakl's poems, in fragments we are left to assemble. I think the narrative is in the images. As the poem opens almost cinematically, from mountains and eagles to green flowers, we sense a closing of perspective, then come to the torrents and gorges of the second stanza, which turn into vestibules and the invocation of family figures. These vestibules symbolically suggest homes and houses, where we hear about the anger of the fathers (not a singular father, but all fathers!) and the sad cries of the mothers (ditto!), and the boy's (singular!) battle cry. And then the conclusion of the stanza, where something is being birthed, something that is "Groaning with blind eyes." What? We don't know; it is unborn, a thing alive enough only to groan.

Whatever is going on here, all the fathers and all the mothers are caught up in the same reactions of anger and sadness, while the boy fights back. Does he fight them, struggle with them? It looks that way, but we cannot be sure. Perhaps he fights at the world thus created, full of angry fathers and lamenting mothers and white voices and homes that are really wild mountains in storm. We get a hint of some such possibility with the image in the first stanza of the "black lambs on the abyss," where the blue goes mute and the silence is like a green plant. In Trakl, as mentioned earlier, blue is a special color, the color of beginnings and endings, that is, the color of pre-dawn and dusk. In this formulation, the beginnings and endings of things are suddenly silent, which I take to mean that they are unjudging and neutral, as a tarnished innocence perches over the abyss (for how else should we construe that black lamb?).

The third and fourth stanzas carry this sense of the violent correspondence of inner and outer worlds further, in the third stanza with the "black tumult / Of horses & carriages" finding an equal weight with "The rose terrible bolt of lightning" in the spruce, and the "burning sorrow / Of an angry God." In the fourth stanza the wild streams become tears and the pity of the storm joins the mountains. Notice how these two stanzas join, how the burning sorrow of the angry God joins to the fire that purifies the night. One might construct a conclusion to this poem that says that in this house which is a mountain filled with storms of angry fathers, lamenting mothers, and an unborn blind thing which is groaning not into this life but only into a significance, the only release possible for the son with his battle-cry in the world of tears he lives in, and for this angry God who oversees it, is this purifying and perhaps divine fire.

Others will find other significances and correspondences in the poem. This is a poem that encourages us to see and to move with them.

Trakl wrote this poem in the same May to early July period that produced several extraordinary works, including "Das Herz" ("The Heart), "Der Schlaf" ("Sleep"), "Der Abend" ("Evening"), "Die Nacht" ("Night"), "Die Schwermut" ("Melancholy"), and "Die Heimkehr" ("Homecoming"). Later would come the masterpieces "Grodek" and "Klage," about World War I, written just before his death. They are wonderful and important poems, but I think this poem marked another turning point in the development of his extraordinary art.

You can see in these poems, and the poems he was yet to write, the impending sense of loss and of the fear and terror of the war that would begin in August of that year. The proximate trigger for World War I was the assassination of Archduke Franz Ferdinand of Austria and his wife Sophie in June, 1914. But an arms race had begun well before this—in 1908-1913, military spending of the European powers increased by fifty per cent, and there was a first and then a second Balkan War, with territories lost and gained, and great powers maneuvering for influence. Bosnia and Herzegovina were called the "powder keg of Europe." War and the talk of war were everywhere, and reading these poems you can feel the poet's sense of doom and even of apocalypse, as he feels around him a world sliding inexorably toward bloody conflict. This sense of fear and dread is even more present in the terrifying war poem, "In The East," the odd and lovely and desolate "Homecoming," and a first version of "Lament." This is not the famous "Klage," one of Trakl's last poems, but neither is it an early version. It stands on its own. All of these poems were published in the magazine Brenner in 1914-1915.

Revelation & Decline

Trakl's four mature prose poems written after 1913 all use the new style begun in "Psalm" and "Helian." The four are: "Verwandlung des Bösen" ("Transformation of Evil"), "Winternacht"("Winter Night"), "Traum und Umnachtung" ("Dream & Madness"), and "Offenbarung und Untergang" ("Revelation & Decline"). The latter two are especially rich in imagery and astounding in the way they develop, finding hidden passageways between images and ideas, but all are strange and mysterious, fragmentary narratives that hint at a greater story lurking just beyond what we can easily see. As with all things that hint of narrative, once we are swept up in it, once we engage, we take over from what the poem has given us and create the sense of completeness ourselves—it's something we insist on mentally as thinking and listening or reading human beings, a sense of sequence and cohesion, a response more intense perhaps in prose than poetry. That sense of cohesion is a necessary element given the length and speed of development of these prose poems. Absent the sense of a story being told, the train of images would be chaotic, and even disorienting, and the poems would fail, on their own terms, and on ours.

The narrative of "Revelation & Decline" appears to center on a dream of the sister, in a world where death is the undertext, and where incest, or the threat of it, is a constant mental companion, an ongoing source of guilt that cannot be expunged, and from which the only escape is a plunge into the abyss. The poem opens with a vision of the world inhabited by dreamers. Everyone is asleep, their rooms are stone, the light that each person has is small, motionless. The narrator dreams that he is sleepwalking through it, an orphan whose father has died, a notion stated in one of the most beautiful lines in the poem: "In this hour of the death of my father I was the white son."

The speaker is haunted by dreams of his own madness and of the dead sister, and of his guilt, which is causeless but real. There is death around him, bitterness in the world, storms, blood, a dead horse–what does he have to do with any of this? Did he cause it? Are these merely tokens of a world he lives in, or markers of any interior nightmare Or— as as these are not exclusive options—both? The poem is extraordinarily rich, very beautiful, and haunting. We can feel the truth of it without necessarily knowing why, at every moment, it is true.

I want to end these comments here. I have tried to show how I read and engage the poems. I do not think that these are the only ways into the poems, and I hope that other readers will find their own methods, and their own vocabularies for discussing these extraordinarily rich poems. I wish all well, and hope these comments are helpful.

5.

Trakl's work has had an interesting publication history, reception, and influence. In his lifetime, only his *Gedichte* (*Poems*) was published, in 1913. In 1915, the year after his death the extraordinary *Sebastian im Traum* (*Sebastian in Dream*) was published, a volume he had prepared prior to his suicide. Both books proved popular, and in 1918 his publisher brought out a collected poems. As his fame grew, translations appeared in Czech, Rumanian, and English in the 1920's, and musical settings of some of the poems were published in 1922 by Paul Hindemith. Appreciation of his work was wide, though there was not much critical commentary or deep analysis, perhaps because the poems seem to travel directly into our appreciation and sensibility without much room for the usual kinds of critical analysis. In fact, there was not much deep critical commentary on Trakl until the 1950's. Interest grew markedly with the publication in 1961 of *Twenty Poems of Georg Trakl* by Robert Bly and James Wright (Sixties Press, Madison, 1961). Bly and Wright, as they seemed to do with many other poets, sparked a real interest in Trakl.

I am grateful for the wonderful translation work done by many others, including Robert Grenier, Michael Hamburger, David Luke, Christopher Middleton, Robert Firmage, Daniel Simko, and Herbert Lindenberger. All have made incisive and useful comments which have helped me and many others enter and love these poems. I single out for praise here not only the work done by Herbert Lindenberger, whose book *Georg Trakl* (Twane Publishers, 1971) influenced many of my readings, but also the invaluable online translations of the work available from Jim Doss and Werner Schmitt, along with the original of the poems.

— Bob Herz 2016

Bibliography

Books I used or consulted in developing these translations and comments:

Herbert Lindenberger, *Georg Trakl* (Twayne Publishers, Inc., 1971)

Robert Formage, *Song of there West Selected Poems of Georg Trakl* (North Point Press, 1988)

Robert Grenier, Michael Hamburger, David Luke, and Christopher Middleton, *Selected Poems Georg Trakl* (Jonathan Cape, 1968)

Daniel Simko, *Autumn Sonata Georg Trakl* (Moyer Bell Limited, 1989)

Allen Hoey, *Transfigured Autumn* (Tamarack Editions, 1984)

James Wright and Robert Bly, *Twenty Poems of Geog Trakl* (Sixties Press, 1961

Jim Doss and Werner Schmitt, *Index of all literary texts of Georg Trakl* (online at http://www.literaturnische.de/Trakl/english/texte-e.htm#seb)

I am also grateful to my brother, Professor Randall Herz, for looking over these translations and attempting to correct some of the more obvious errors. It goes without saying, I hope, that all errors are mine.

I

Aphorisms & Fragments

Aphorisms & Fragments

1.
Wisdom only to one who scorns happiness.

2.
What passes silently under autumn trees
Near the green river, while gulls glide above—
Falling of leaves; simplicity of dark times.
It is God's peace. The evening shadows linger.
A black bird sings in the autumn trees.

The hands folded as for prayer weary & harmonious
Evening & the eyes follow the omen birds
Before surrendering to dream memories
Of the boy so delicate so slight.

A black bird sings in autumn trees
The peace of days so vast so sweet
The soul also silently prepares itself.

3.
The cross looms up Elis
Your body on darkening paths

4.
Birth

Walk with the father, walk with the mother

5.
>   In Spring
Evening has come to the ancient garden

6.
(Nocturnal Metamorphosis, Death & Spirit)

When I collapsed on the black hill of Sleep
weary of the wild land & the desperation of bleak winterdays,
the vision came to me suddenly on glowing wing:

7.
As the sun sank away K. departed

8.
The Homeless One returns
To moss-grown forests

9.
Munch woke at the edge of the wood toward evening. A
gold cloud faded above him & the dark peace of autumn
filled him with fear. Everywhere around him the solitariness of hills.

10.
Spring; a frail corpse
Shining in its grave
Among the wild
Elder-bushes of childhood.

11.
Beech-trees of night; a red worm
Lives in the heart's dark country.

12.
Snowy night!
Dark sleepers
Under the bridge
Crystal sweat that falls
From your shattered brow

II

The Breakthrough

Psalm (2nd Version)

There is a light the wind blows out,
There is a tavern the village drunkard leaves in the afternoon,
There are holes filled with spiders in the black scorched vineyard,
There is a room they have whitewashed with milk.
One day the Mad One died. There is an island in the South Seas
That will receive the Sun-God. When the drums sound,
The men begin their war-dances.
The women shake their hips covered in vines & poppies
When the ocean sings. O lost paradise!

The nymphs leave their forests of gold.
They bury the Stranger. A glistening rain begins.
The son of Pan appears as a common laborer
Who sleeps through noon on the burning asphalt.
There are young girls in the courtyard in dresses of heart-rending
    poverty!
There are rooms filled with chords & sonatas.
There are shadows that embrace in front of a blind mirror.
The sick warm themselves at the hospital windows.
A white steamer carries the bloody pestilence up the canal.

The strange sister appears again in someone's evil dream.
Resting in the hazel-bush she toys with his stars.
The student, or perhaps his double, gazes after her a long time from
    the window.
Behind him stands the dead brother, or he descends the worn
    winding-stairs.
In the dark of the chestnut-trees, the figure of the young novice grows
    pale.
It is evening in the garden. Commotion of bats in the cloister.

The children of the caretaker stop their play & seek the gold of heaven.
Final chord of a quartet. The little blind girl runs trembling through the avenue,
Later her shadow gropes along cold walls, surrounded by fairy- tales & holy legends.

There is an empty boat that drifts down the black canal at evening.
Human ruins decay in the dusk of the old asylum.
The dead orphans lay on the garden wall.
Angels with filth-stained wings step from gray walls.
Maggots fall from their yellowed eyelids.
The square in front of the church is dark & silent, as in the days of childhood.
Former lives glide past on silver feet
& the shadows of the damned sink down to groaning waters.
In his grave the white magician toys with his serpents.

Silently God's gold eyes open over Golgotha.

Helian

I
In the lonely hours of the spirit
It is beautiful to walk in the sun
Along the yellow walls of summer.
The footsteps soft in the grass; still
The son of Pan sleeps on in gray marble.

Evenings on the terrace we used to get drunk on brown wine.
The peach has a red glow in the leaves;
Gentle sonata, happy laughter.

The night-quiet is beautiful.
On a dark plain
We meet shepherds & white stars.

When autumn comes
There is a sober clarity in the grove.
We walk along the red walls, calm now,
& our round eyes follow the flights of the birds.
In the evening, white water sinks in the funeral urns.

The sky rests in bare branches.
The peasant carries bread & wine in pure hands
& the fruit ripens peacefully in a sunny room.

How solemn the faces of the beloved dead.
Yet the soul delights in righteous contemplation.

II
How powerful the silence of the ruined garden,
When the young novice garlands his forehead with brown leaves,
& with his breath drinks in the icy gold.

Hands touch against the age of blue waters
Or on a cold night the white cheeks of the sisters.

The walk past friendly rooms is quiet & harmonious,
Where there is solitude & the rustle of the maple,
Where the thrush, perhaps, still sings.

Man is beautiful, shining in the darkness,
When amazed, he moves his arms & legs,
& his eyes roll silently in their purple caves.

At vespers, the stranger loses his way in the black destruction of
    November,
Under branches that are rotting, along walls full of leprosy,
Where once the holy brother walked,
Absorbed in the soft string music of his madness.

How lonely the evening wind when it ends.
Slowly dying, the head sinks in the dark of the olive tree.

III
The ruin of a generation is shattering.
In this hour, the eyes of the one who watches fill
With the gold of his stars.

Evening, & the bells that no longer ring sink down,
The black walls on the town-square fall to ruin,
The dead soldier is calling to a prayer.

A pale angel,
The son enters the empty house of his fathers.

The sisters have gone far away to white old men.
At night the sleeper found them under the pillars in the entrance-hall,
Returned from their sad pilgrimages.

How stiff their hair from filth & worms,
As he stands there with silver feet,
& these dead ones emerge from bare rooms.

You psalms that come in the fiery rain of midnight,
When the servants beat the gentle eyes with brambles,
& the childlike fruits of the elderberry
Bow astonished over the empty grave.

Softly the yellow moons roll
Over the fever-sheets of the youth,
Until even the silence of winter follows him.

IV
A great destiny thinks its way down the Kidron River,
Where the cedar, the gentle creature,
Opens under the blue brows of the father.
At night a shepherd leads his flock across the meadow.
Or there are cries in sleep,
When the bronze angel approaches the man in the grove,
& the saint's flesh melts away on the fiery grate.

The purple vines climb around huts of mud,
The yellow grain sounds in its sheaves,
There is the humming of bees, the flight of the crane.
At night those who have risen from the dead meet on rocky paths.

The lepers are reflected in the black waters;
Or they open their filthy robes
Crying to the fragrant wind that blows from the rosy hill.

The thin servant-girls grope through the alleyways of night,
To find the shepherd of love.
On Saturdays, gentle singing in the huts.

Let the song also remember the boy,
His madness, & his white brow & his final departure,
The ruined one, who opens his blue eyes.
How sad to meet again like this.

V
In black rooms, steps of madness,
Shadows of old men under the open door,
As Helian's soul looks at itself in the rosy mirror
& snow & leprosy sink from his brow.

On the walls the stars are extinguished
& the white figures of the light.

The grave-remnants rise from the carpets,
The silence of decayed crosses on the hill,
The incense sweet in the purple of the night-wind.

You shattered eyes in black mouths,
When the grandson in his gentle night-madness
Thinks of the darker end in solitude,
The silent god lowers his blue lids over him.

III

Sebastian In Dream

Section 1: Sebastian in Dream

Childhood

The elder full of fruit; childhood has dwelled calmly
In a blue cave. Silent branches ponder
Over the old path where wild grass waves
& has turned brown; the rustle of leaves

Makes a sound like blue water in stone.
Soft lament of the blackbirds. A shepherd
Silently follows the sun as it rolls down the autumnal hill.

A blue moment is only more soul.
A shy deer appears at the forest's edge & peacefully
Old bells & sinister hamlets rest in the valley.

More devout now, you know the meaning of the dark years,
Coolness & autumn in lonely rooms;
& the shining footsteps that ring forth continuously in the holy
      blueness.

An open window rattles its a small sound; tears flow
At the sight of the ruined cemetery by the hill,
Memories of legends told over & over; but the soul sometimes
      brightens
Thinking of happier people, of dark-gold spring days.

Song of Hours

The lovers look at each other with dark eyes,
The blonde, radiant ones. Dark & rigid,
Their thin yearning arms entwine.

Purple broke the blessed mouth. Round eyes
Mirroring the dark gold of the spring afternoon,
Edge & blackness of the forest, evening-fear in the green;
Perhaps the unspeaking flight of birds, the unborn's
Path past sinister villages those lonely summers ago,
& sometimes the decayed blueness releases a shape taken from us.

The yellow corn rustles quietly in the field.
Life is hard & the farmer swings the scythe,
The carpenter joins the big rafters.

The leaves turn purple in fall; the monastic spirit
Wanders through serene days; the grape is ripe
& the air festive in spacious courtyards.
The yellowed fruits smell sweeter; laughter
Is quiet, there is music & dance in shady cellars;
In the twilit garden the step & stillness of the dead boy.

On The Road

In the evening they carried the stranger into the chamber of the dead;
A smell of tar; quiet rustling of red sycamores;
The dark flight of crows; a guard took his station in the square.
The sun has sunk in black linens; the past evening returns again &
    again.
In the next room, the sister plays a Schubert sonata.
Very quietly her smile sinks into the ruined fountain
Which murmurs bluish in the dusk. O how old is our race.
Someone whispers down in the garden; someone has left this black
    sky.
There is the scent of apples on the cabinet. Grandmother lights golden
    candles.

O, how mild is the autumn. Quiet sound of our steps in the old park
Among the tall trees. O, how serious is hyacinth face of dusk.
The blue spring by your feet, the mysterious red silence of your
    mouth,
Shadowed by the slumber of leaves, the dark gold of decayed
    sunflowers.
Your eyelids are heavy from poppy & dream softly on my forehead.
Soft bells tremble through the breast. A blue cloud,
Your face has fallen over me in the dusk.

A song with guitar, heard in a strange inn,
The wild elder bushes there, a long past November day,
Familiar steps on the dusky staircase, sight of brown rafters,
An open window where a sweet hope lingered—
All this so unspeakable, God, that we fall on our knees, shaken.

O, how dark is this night. A purple flame
Failed at my mouth. In the stillness,

The lonely string music of the anxious soul fades & dies.
Let it be. Drunk on wine, the head sinks into the gutter.

Landscape

September evening; the dark calls of the shepherds sound sad
Through the dusky village; fire sparks in the forge.
A huge black horse rears up; the hyacinthine locks of the maid
Seek the fervor of his purple nostrils. Quietly the call of the doe
Makes the edge of the forest seem more solid
& the yellow flowers of autumn
Bend without speaking over the blue face of the pond.
A tree that burns in red flame. Commotion of the dark faces of bats.

To The Boy Elis

When the blackbird calls in the black wood,
Elis, this is your descent.
You drink the coolness of the blue rock-spring.

When your forehead gently bleeds
Give up the ancient legends
& the dark interpretations of the bird's flight.

But you walk softly into the night,
Where the grapes hang full & purple,
& you move your arms more beautifully in the blue.

The thorn-bush sounds
Where your moonlike eyes are.
How long, Elis, you have been dead.

Your body is a hyacinth,
The monk dips his waxen fingers into it.
Our silence is a black cave,

Sometimes a gentle animal steps out of it
& slowly lowers his heavy lids.
A black dew gathers at your temples,

It is the final gold of the ruined stars.

Elis

1.
How perfect the stillness of this golden day.
Under the ancient oaks
You, Elis, appear in perfect repose with your round eyes.

Their blueness that mirrors the sleep of lovers.
On your mouth
Their rosy love-sighs were silenced.

Evening & the fisherman pulled in the heavy nets.
The good shepherd
Leads his herd along the forest's edge.
How righteous your days, Elis.

The blue stillness
Of olive-trees sinks softly along bare walls,
Gently the mysterious song of the old man dies away.

The golden boat
That is your heart, Elis, trembles in a lonely heaven.

2.
The bells sound softly in Elis' breast
In the evening,
When his head sinks into the black cushion.

    The blue deer
Bleeds gently in the thorn bush.

A brown tree stands alone there, dead;
The blue fruits fell from it.

Signs & stars
Disappear softly into the night pond.

It is winter behind the hill.

At night
Blue doves drink the icy sweat
That falls from Elis' crystal brow.

God's lonely wind sounds endlessly along black walls.

Hohenburg

No one in the house. Autumn in all the rooms;
Moon-bright sonata
& the awakening edge of the twilit forest.

You always imagine the white face of man
Far from the turmoil of time;
Over a dreaming shape tending the green branches,

Cross & evening;
His star embraces with purple arms the one who makes sounds
Climbing up to uninhabited windows.

Thus the stranger trembles in his darkness
& quietly lifts his eyelids over a distant human shape;
There is the silver voice of the wind in the hallway.

Sebastian in Dream

For Adolf Loos

1.
Mother carried the infant in the white moon,
In the shade of the walnut tree, the ancient elder,
Drunk with the sap of the poppy, cry of the thrush;
& silently
A bearded face bent over her in compassion

Quiet in the darkness of the window; & in the old household
The goods of the fathers, ancestral heirlooms,
Lay in decay; love & autumnal reverie.

So dark the day of the year, sad childhood,
The boy quietly walked down to cool waters, silver fishes,
Calm & countenance;
When he threw himself down like a stone to where black horses raced,
In the grey night his star possessed him;

Or when holding his mother's freezing hand
He walked at evening over Saint Peter's autumnal cemetery,
A delicate corpse lay still in the darkness of the bedroom
& raised its cold eyelids over him.

But he was a small bird in bare branches,
The bell rang in the November dusk,
The father's silence, as he descended the twilit sleep of the spiral stair.

2
Peace of the soul. Lonely winter evening,
The dark figures of shepherds at the old pond;
Infant in the hut of straw; how quietly
His face sank in black fever.
O Holy night.

Or holding his father's hard hand
He silently climbed Calvary
& in dusky recesses of the rock
The blue figure of Man passed through his Legend,
Blood ran purple from the wound below the heart.
& the cross rose up quietly in the dark of his soul.

Love; when in black corners the snow melted,
A blue breeze was caught cheerfully in the old elder,
In the shadowy vault made by the walnut tree;
& quietly a rosy angel appeared to the boy.

Pleasure; as in cool rooms the sounds of an evening sonata,
In the brown rafters
A blue moth crept from its silver chrysalis.

O nearness of death. From the stony wall
A yellow head bent down, silencing the child,
When in that March the moon decayed & fell.

3
Rose-color of the Easter Bell in the burial vault of night
& the silver voices of the stars,
So that in showers dark insanity fell from the sleeper's brow.

O how silent a walk down the blue river,
Thinking about things forgotten, when from green branches
The thrush calls a stranger to this world of ruin.

Or when holding the old man's bony hand
He walked in the evening before the ruined wall of the city,
Carrying a rose infant in his black greatcoat,
& in the shadow of the walnut tree the spirit of evil appeared.

Groping his way over the green steps of summer. How softly
The garden decayed in the brown stillness of autumn,
Scent & melancholy of the old elder,
As in Sebastian's shadow the silver voice of the angel died.

On the Moor

Wanderer in black wind; the dry reed whispers
In the stillness of the moor. A flock
Of wild birds follows across the gray sky,
Crossing above dark waters.

Turmoil & revolt. In decayed huts
The rot flutters up with black wings;
The crippled birches sigh in the wind.

Evening in the deserted tavern. The way home
Scented by the gentle melancholy of grazing herds,
Nocturnal apparition: toads plunging from silver waters.

In Spring

Quietly snow fell from the dark steps,
In the shadow of the tree
Lovers lift their rosy eyelids.

Always star & night
Follow the mariners' dark calls;
& the oars beat quietly in time.

Soon violets will bloom
On the decayed wall
& green become the silent temple of the lonely.

Evening in Lans

Wanderings through the summer twilight
Past bundles of yellowed corn. We drank the fiery wine
Beneath whitewashed arches, where the swallow flew in & out.

Beautiful: O melancholy & purple laughter.
Evening & the dark scents of green
Cool our burning brows with showers.

Silver waters running down the steps of the forest,
Night & mute, a forgotten life.
Friend; the leafy footpaths to the village.

At the Mönchsberg

Where the crumbling path descends in the shadow of autumnal elms,
Far from the leafy huts, the sleeping shepherds,
The dark figure of coolness always follows the wanderer

Over the footbridge of bone, the hyacinthine voice of the boy,
Quietly telling the forgotten legend of the forest,
& more softly, a sick shape now, the wild lament of the brother.

Thus a little bit of green touches the knee of the stranger,
& the head that has turned to stone;
Nearer, the blue spring murmurs the cries of the women.

Kaspar Hauser Song

To Bessie Loos

He truly loved the sun, as it descended crimson down the hill,
The paths of the forest, the singing blackbird,
& the joy of green.

Serious was his dwelling in the shadow of the tree
& pure his face.
God spoke a soft flame to his heart:
O man!

Silently his footstep found the city in the evening;
His dark lament:
I want to be a horseman.

But bush & beast pursued him,
House & the twilit garden of pallid humans
& his murderer searched for him.

Spring & summer & beautiful autumn
Of the righteous one, his quiet step
Past the dark rooms of dreamers.
At night he remained alone with his star;

Saw the snow that fell through the bare branches
& in the murky hallway the shadow of his murderer.

Silverly it sank, the head of something not yet born.

At Night

The blueness of my eyes has gone out in this night,
The red gold of my heart. How silently the light burned.
Your blue coat surrounded the one who was falling;
Your red mouth sealed the madness of the Friend.

Metamorphosis of Evil

Autumn: black below the forest's edge; Minute of mute destruction; the brow of the leper under the barren tree. It is long past evening, which descends over the steps of moss; November. A bell tolls & the shepherd leads a herd of black & red horses into the village. Under the hazel bush, the green hunter disembowels a wild animal. His hands smoke with blood & the shade of the deer sighs in leaves over his eyes, which are brown & taciturn; the forest. Crows that scatter; three. Their flight resembles a sonata of faded chords & masculine gloom; a gold cloud gently dissolves. Near the mill, boys light a fire. Flame is the palest brother, & its laughs are buried in his purple hair; or it is a place of murder which a hard path leads past. The barberries are gone, & in the long year one dreams in leaden air under the pines. Fear, green darkness, gurgling of a drowning man: from out of the starry pond the fisherman pulls a large black fish, its face full of cruelty & madness. The voices of the reed, of quarreling men behind them, in a red boat one who sways wildly across the freezing waters of autumn, living in the dark legends of his race, & the eyes opened like stone over the nights & virgin terrors. Evil.

What makes you stand silently on the ruined stair in the house of your fathers? Leaden blackness. What do you raise with your silver hand to your eyes, & the eyes sinking away as if drunk from poppy? But you see the starry heaven through the stone wall, the Milky Way, Saturn; red. Raging, the barren tree knocks against the stone wall. You, on decayed steps: tree, star, stone! You, a blue animal trembling quietly; you, the pale priest who butchers it on the black altar. Your smile in the darkness, sad & angry, so that a child turns pale in its sleep. A red flame from your hand burned up a moth. The flute of light, the flute of death. What made you stand silently on the ruined stair in the house of your fathers? Below, at the gate, an angel knocks with crystalline finger.

O hell of sleep; dark alley, small brown garden. The dead woman rings quietly in the blue evening. Green flowers all around & her face is gone. Or it fades & bends over the cold brow of the murderer in the dark hall; adoration, purple flame of desire. Dying, crashing over the black levels of sleepers in the darkness.

Someone left you at the the crossroad & you look back for a long time. Silver step in the shadow of stunted apple trees. Purple fruit shines in black branches & the snake molts in the grass. O! the darkness; sweat that breaks out on the icy brow, & sad dreams from the wine, in the village inn, under smoke-blackened rafters. You, still the savage conjuring up rosy islands in clouds of brown tobacco smoke, & drawing from your inner self the raptor's wild cry as it hunts around black cliffs in sea, storm & ice. You, green metal & inside a fiery face that wants to sing away the sinister ages & the angel's flaming fall. O! Despair, that falls to the knee with a mute cry.

A dead man visits you. The self-split blood runs from the heart & an unspeakable moment nests in the black brow; dark encounter. You—a purple moon when the other appears in the green shadow of the olive tree. Everlasting night follows after.

Section 2: Autumn of the Lonely

In the Park

Again wandering the old park,
Silence of yellow & red flowers.
You also mourn, you gentle gods,
& the autumn gold of the elm.
Reeds are motionless over the blue pond
The thrush silent in the evening.
O bend your forehead before
The ruined marble of the ancestors.

A Winter Evening

When snow falls against the window,
The evening bell rings long,
The table is prepared for many,
& the house is well ordered.

Many come to this gate from
Long wanderings on dark paths.
The tree of grace blooms in gold
From the cool sap of the earth.

In the stillness the Wanderer steps inside;
Grief has worn the threshold to stone.
But there shines in the pure light,
On the table, the Bread & Wine.

The Cursed

1
 At twilight the old women go to the well.
There is red laughter in the darkness of the chestnuts.
There is the smell of bread from a shop
& there are sunflowers falling over the fence.

By the river the inn still sounds mild & quiet.
There is the sound of a guitar, jingling of money.
There is a halo on that small child who waits
Gently and white at the glass door.

She awakens a blue radiance in the panes,
Framed by thorns, black & rapturous.
A crooked writer smiles crazily
Into water, starting a sudden tumult.

2
In the evening, plague trims her blue garment
& quietly a melancholy guest closes the door.
The black burden of the maple falls across the window;
A boy places his forehead in her hand.

Often her eyelids will droop, evil & heavy.
The child's hands comb through her hair
& his tears fall hot & clear into
The sockets of her eyes that are black & empty.

A nest of scarlet snakes writhes
Lethargically in her troubled womb.
Her arms release a thing that has died,
That is surrounded by the carpet's sadness.

3
A chime sounds in the brown garden.
There is a blueness in the darkness of the chestnut trees,
The sweet coat of a strange woman.
Fragrant scent of mignonettes; & a glowing sense

Of evil. The damp brow bends cold & pale
Over the garbage where the rat digs,
Washed by the mild scarlet shine of stars;
Apples fall with a gentle sound in the garden.

The night is black. The night wind billows out
The white nightgown of the sleepwalking boy
As quietly the dead hand reaches to touch his mouth.
The smile of Sonja is gentle & beautiful.

Sonja

Evening returns in the old garden.
Sonja's life, blue stillness.
The migrations of wild birds;
Bare tree in autumn silence.

Sunflower, softly bent
Over Sonja's white life.
The red wound, never shown,
Only lives in dark rooms,

Where the blue bells ring;
Sonja's step & gentle stillness.
The greeting of a dying animal as it passes away,
Bare tree in autumn silence.

The sun of ancient days shines
Over Sonja's white forehead,
Snow that moistens her cheeks
& the wilderness of her brow.

Along

Now grain & grape are cut,
The hamlet in autumn & rest.
Hammer & anvil sound incessantly,
There is laughter in the crimson bower.

Bring the asters from dark fences
To the white child.
Say how long we've been in dying;
The sun will shortly rise in black.

Red fish in the pond;
This fear of hearing one's own thoughts;
The evening wind blows softly at the window,
There is the organ's blue singsong.

Star & secret glittering
Let you raise your eyes once more.
The mother appears in pain & horror;
Black mignonettes in the darkness.

Autumn Soul

Hunter's calls & the bloody baying;
Behind cross & brown hill
Placidly the pond-mirror blinds,
The hawk's cries are hard & bright.

A black silence already trembles
Over stubble field & path;
Pure sky in the branches;
Only the brook runs still & calm.

Fish & deer soon slip away.
Blue soul, dark wandering
Separates us so quickly from loved ones & others.
Evening changes the sense & image of things.

A life of righteous Bread & Wine,
Places God into your mild hands
Man creates the dark end,
Filled with guilt & red punishment.

Afra

A child with brown hair. Prayer & Amen
Silently darken the evening coolness
& Afra's smile, red in a yellow frame
Of sunflowers, fear & grey sultriness.

The monk saw her in ages past. wrapped in blue cloak,
Devoutly painted in church windows;
Even in pain this friendship can be a friendly guide
When his blood is haunted by her stars.

Autumn decline; & the silence of the elder-trees.
The water's blue motion stirs the forehead,
A cloth of hair is laid carefully on a bier.

Rotten fruits fall from the branches;
An unspeakable flight of birds, meeting
The dying; after this all the dark years follow.

Autumn of the Lonely

Dark autumn returns full of fruit & plenty,
The yellow sheen of beautiful summer days.
A pure blue flows from the dull ruined shells;
The flight of birds carries sounds from old legends.
The wine is pressed, the mild stillness
Is filled with quiet answers to dark questions.

Here & there, a cross on barren hills;
In the red forest a herd has wandered off.
Clouds mirrored in the surface of the pond;
There is a calmness in the gestures of the farmer.
Very quietly the blue wing of evening stirs
Over the roof of dried straw, the black earth.

Soon the stars will nest in the brows of the weary one;
In cool rooms a silent modesty enters
& angels step quietly from the blue eyes
Of the lovers, whose suffering grows gentle.
The reed rustles; there is a bony horror that comes
When the black dew drips from barren pastures.

Section 3: Seven-song of Death

Rest & Silence

Shepherds buried the sun in the bare forest.
A fisherman
Pulled in the moon in a net of hair from the freezing pond.

The pale man
Lives in blue crystal, cheek leaning against his stars;
Or bows his head in purple sleep.

But the black flight of birds always
Touches the one who gazes after, the sanctity of blue flowers,
The near stillness recalling forgotten things, extinct angels.

Once again the forehead darkens in rocks from the moon.
A radiant youth appears,
It is the sister in autumn & black decay.

Anif

Remembrance: gulls gliding across the dark sky
Of male melancholy.
Silently you live in the shadow of the autumn ash-tree,
Sunk into the righteous measure of the hill;

Always you walk down the green river,
At evening,
Sounding love; peacefully encountering the dark prey,

A rosy man; drunk with blue weather
His forehead stirs the dying leaves
& think of the serious face of the mother;
How everything sinks into darkness;

The austere rooms & old goods
Of the fathers.
This shakes the breast of the stranger.
O signs & stars.

The guilt of those who have been born is very great. Woe to you
Golden shivers of death
When the soul dreams of cooler blossoms.

Always the night bird cries in the bare branches
Over the steps of the moonlit one,
An icy wind sounds along the village walls.

Birth

Mountains: blackness, silence & snow.
The hunt descends red from the forest.
O, mossy gazes of the prey.

The silence of the mother; among the black pines
Sleeping hands open
When the moon appears, cold & decayed.

O birth of man. At night blue water
Rushes over the rocky ground;
Sighing, the fallen angel sees his image,

A pale shape awakens in a musty room.
the eyes
Of the stony old woman shine, two moons.

The cry of a woman in labor. The night
Touches the boy's temple with black wings,
Snow falls quietly from a purple cloud.

Decline

To Karl Borromaeus Heinrich

Over the white pond
The wild birds have gone.
At evening an icy wind blows from our stars.

The shattered forehead of night
Leans down over our graves.
We sway beneath the oaks in a silver boat.

The white walls of the city resound constantly.
Under arches of thorns
O my brother we are blind hands climbing toward midnight.

To One Who Died Young

O, the black angel who stepped quietly from the heart of the tree
When we were gentle playmates in the evening
At the edge of the bluish fountain.
Our step was quiet, big eyes in the brown coolness of autumn,
The purple sweetness of the stars.

But the other one descended the stone steps of the Mönchsberg,
A blue smile on his face & strangely cocooned
In his silent childhood, & died;
The silver face of his friend stayed behind in the garden,
Listening in the leaves or in ancient stones.

The soul sang of death, the green rot of the flesh
& it was the murmur of the forest,
The fervent lament of the animals.
Always the blue bells of evening rang from the twilight towers.

The hour came when the other saw the shadows in the purple sun,
The shadows of decay in the bare branches;
At evening, when the blackbird sang by the twilit wall,
The ghost of the one who had died young silently appeared in the
    room.

O, the blood that runs from the throat of the singer,
Blue flower; o fiery tear
Wept into the night.

Golden cloud & time. In a lonely chamber
You invite the dead one to visit more often,
You wander in intimate conversation under the elms down by the
    green river.

Spiritual Twilight

Silently the dark prey is met at the edge
Of the forest;
At the hill the evening breeze dies quietly,

The cry of the blackbird grows mute
& the soft flutes of autumn
Are silent in the reeds.

On a black cloud
You travel drunk with the poppy
The night-pond,

The starry sky.
The moonlit voice of the sister sounds constantly
Through the spiritual night.

Song of the West

O the nocturnal wing beat of the soul:
Shepherds once, we walked in twilit forests
& the red deer, the green flower & the murmuring spring
Humbly followed. O, the ancient sound of the cricket,
The blood blooming on the sacrificial altar stone,
& the cry of a lonely bird above the green stillness of the pond.

O, you crusades & glowing tortures
Of the flesh, the fall of the crimson fruit
In the garden at evening, where long ago the pious disciples walked,
Soldiers now, waking from wounds & star-dreams.
O, the gentle cornflower sheaf of night.

O, periods of silence & golden autumns,
When we peaceful monks made the purple wine,
& hill & forest shone all around us.
O, hunts & castles; peace of evening,
When in his chamber man pondered Justice,
& struggled in mute prayer for the living Godhead.

O, the bitter hour of decline,
When we behold a stone face in black water.
But the radiant lovers lift their silver eyelids:
They are one kin now. Incense flows from the rosy pillows
& the sweet song of those risen from the dead.

Transfiguration

When evening appears
A blue face quietly leaves you.
A small bird sings in the tamarind tree.

A soft monk
Folds the deadened hands.
A white angel haunts Mary.

A nocturnal wreath
Of violets, grain, & purple grapes
Is the year of the watcher.

The graves of the dead
Open by your feet
When you lay your forehead into your silver hands.

Silently the autumn moon
Dwells upon your mouth,
A dark song drunk with poppy juice;

Blue flower,
That quietly sounds in yellowed rocks.

South Wind

Blind cries of the wind, moonlike days of winter,
Childhood, steps softly fading near black hedge,
Long toll of evening bells.
Softly the white night comes,

To transform into purple dreams the pain & affliction
Of a stony life,
So that the thorny sting will never leave the rotting body.

Deep in slumber, the anxious soul heaves a sigh,

& the wind deep in broken trees,
& the the mother, lamenting,
Staggers through the lonely forest

Of this speechless grief; nights
Filled with tears, fiery angels.
A silver childlike skeleton shatters against a bare wall.

The Wanderer

Always the white night leaning on the hill,
Where poplars stand in silver tones,
Stars & stones.

Asleep, the footbridge arches over the torrent,
The face of the dead one follows the boy,
Crescent moon in a rosy gorge

Far from the eulogizing shepherds. In ancient rocks
The toad looks out of crystal eyes,
& the blossoming breeze awakens, the birdcall of the dead peers,
& the footsteps quietly turn green in the forest.

This is reminiscent of tree & animal. Slow stages of moss;
& the moon,
That sinks glowing into melancholy waters.

He returns again & roams the green shores,
Sways wildly in a black gondola through the ruined city.

Karl Kraus

White high priest of truth,
Crystalline voice in which dwells the icy breath of God,
Angry magician,
Under whose flaming coat rattles the blue armor of the warrior.

To the Silenced

O, madness of the great city at evening,
When the stunted trees stand rigid at the black wall,
& the spirit of evil gazes from a silver mask;
Light displaces the stony night with a magnetic scourge.
O, the sunken tolling of evening bells.

Whore, who with icy shudders gives birth to a dead child.
Raging, God's fury whips the brow of the one possessed,
Crimson pestilence, hunger that breaks green eyes.
O, horrible laughter of gold.

But humanity silently bleeds in dark caves,
& assembles the redeeming head from hard metals.

Passion

When Orpheus touches the lute in that silvery way,
To lament a dead thing in the garden of night,
Who are you to be resting under the high trees?
The lament rustles the autumn reeds,
The blue pond,
Dying out under green trees
Following the shadow of the sister;
Dark love
Wild generation,
Day rushes from you on golden wheels.
Silent night.

Under dark firs
Two wolves mix their blood
In a stony embrace; the gold of the cloud
Loses itself over the footpath,
Patience & silence of childhood.
The tender corpse is met again
On Triton pond
Slumbering in its hyacinthine hair.
May that cool head finally implode!

For a blue deer always follows,
Seeking under darkening trees
Darker paths,
Alert & moved by the night songs,
Gentle madness;
Or the dark rapture
Of the lute sounded
To cool the feet of the penitent woman
In the city of stone.

Seven-song of Death

Blue dawn of Spring: under sucking trees
A dark shape wanders into evening & ruin,
Listening to the gentle lament of the blackbird.
Night appears silently, a bleeding deer
That slowly sinks down the hill.

The blossoming apple branches sway in moist air,
Their silver entanglements dissolving,
Dying away in night-dark eyes; falling stars;
Gentle song of childhood.

The sleeper descended the black forest,
& a blue spring murmured from the ground,
Pale eyelids lifted quietly
Over his snowy countenance;

& the moon chased a red animal
From its cave;
& the dark lament of women died in sighs.

The white stranger raised his hands more radiantly
To his star;
Silently the dead thing leaves the ruined house.

O decomposed form of Man: assembled from cold metals,
Night terrors & buried forests
& the scorching wilderness of the animal;
Winds silence of the soul.

In a blackish boat he floated down the shimmering streams,

Filled with purple stars, & the green branches
Sank peacefully over him,
Poppy from silver clouds.

Winter Night

Snow has fallen. After midnight, drunk with purple wine, you leave the dark precinct of Men, the red flame of their hearth. O darkness!

Black frost. The earth is hard, the air bitter. Your stars show evil signs.

With petrified steps you stomp along the railway-embankment, eyes wide, like a soldier storming a black hill. Avanti!

Bitter snow & moon!

A red wolf strangled by an angel. Your legs rattle as you walk like blue ice & a smile of sadness & arrogance turns your face to stone & your forehead grows pale with the lust of frost;

or it leans silently over the sleep of a watchman, sunk in his wooden hut.

Frost & smoke. A white shirt of stars burns the shoulders that wear it & God's vultures mangle your metallic heart.

O the hills of stone. Silent & forgotten, the cool body melts in silver snow.

Black sleep. The ear follows the paths of the stars in the ice for a long time.

Church bells were ringing in the village as you woke. All in silver, the rosy day stepped in from the eastern gate.

Section 4: Song of the Departed

In Venice

Stillness in the nocturnal room.
Silver-like flickering of the candelabra
Before the singing
Of the Lonely One;
Enchanting rose-colored clouds.

Blackish swarm of flies
Darkens the stony room
& the head of the homeless one
Stares from the torment
Of a golden day.

The sea is motionless at night.
Star & blackish travel
Vanished down the canal.
Child, your sickly smile
Followed me quietly in sleep.

Limbo

Shadows search by autumnal walls
For singing gold on the hill
Evening clouds graze
In the peace of withered sycamores.
This age breathes darker tears,
Condemnation, for the dreamer's heart
That overflows with the purple sunset,
& the melancholy of the smoking city;
A golden coolness from the cemetery
Drifts along where the stranger walks,
As if a tender corpse followed in shadow.

The stone building softly rings;
The garden of the orphanage, the dark hospital,
A red boat on the canal.
The decaying men rise & sink
Dreaming in the darkness
& Angels with cold brows
Step out from blackish gates;
Blueness, death keening of mothers.
A wheel of fire rolls through
Their long hair, the round day
Of Earth's torment without end.

In cool meaningless rooms
Furniture & utensils rot, as unholy childhood
Fumbles with bony hands
Into the blue for fairy tales,
The fat rat gnaws at door & trunk,
Heart
Frozen in snowy stillness.

Hunger's purple curses
Echo in the rotting dark,
The black swords of lying,
As if an iron gate slammed shut.

The Sun

Each day the yellow sun comes over the hill.
Beautiful the forest, the dark animal,
Man, hunter or shepherd.

The fish rises reddish in the green pond.
Under round heavens
The fisherman drifts quietly in a blue boat.

The grapes ripen slowly, & the grain.
As the day silently ends
Many things are prepared, both good & evil.

When night comes,
The wanderer quietly lifts his heavy eyes;
The sun breaks from its dark abyss.

Song of a Captive Blackbird

For Ludwig von Ficker

Dark breath in green branches.
Tiny blue flowers hover about the face
Of the lonely one, the golden step
Dying under the olive tree.
Night flutters up on drunken wing.
Humility bleeds so softly,
Dew that drops slowly from a blossoming thorn.
Compassion of radiant arms
That embraces a breaking heart.

Summer

At evening the song of the cuckoo
Is silent in the forest.
The corn bends lower,
The red poppy.

Black storm threatens
Over the hill.
The ancient song of the cricket
Dies in the field.

The leaves of the chestnut
Never stir.
Your dress rustles
On the spiral stair.

Silence lights the candle
In the dark room;
A silver hand
Extinguished it;

Calm & starless night.

End of Summer

The green summer has become so quiet,
Your crystalline countenance.
The flowers died by the evening pond,
The frightened call of a blackbird.

Futile hope of life. At home the swallow
Prepares its journey & the sun
Sets on the hill; already the night
Beckons for its journey by the stars.

Silence of the villages; the deserted forests
Resound all around. Heart,
Bend now more lovingly over
The calm woman who is sleeping.

The green summer has grown so quiet;
& the stranger's step rings
Through the silver night.
Would a blue deer remember this path,

Or the beautiful harmony of its spiritual years!

Year

Dark stillness of childhood. Under the green ash trees
Meekness grazes with bluish looks; golden peace.
A dark thing delights in the scent of violets; swaying ears of corn
At evening, seed & the golden shadows of melancholy.
The carpenter trims the beams; the mill grinds
In the twilit valley; a scarlet mouth arches in the hazel leaves,
A masculine red bent over the silent waters.
Autumn is quiet, the spirit of the forest; a gold cloud
Follows the lonely one; the black shadow of the grandson.
The ending is in a room of stone; under old cypress trees
The nocturnal images of tears are gathered in a well;
Golden eye of the inception, dark patience of the end.

Occident

To Else Lasker-Schüler, with admiration

1
Moon, like a dead thing
From a blue cave,
& the many blossoms falling
On the rock path.
A silverly sick creature weeps
By the evening pond,
The Lovers in a black boat
Died crossing over.

Or the steps of Elis
Ring through the grove,
Hyacinth-filled,
Again under oaks.
O the boy's figure
Carved from crystalline tears,
Nocturnal shadows.
Jagged lightning illuminates the temple,
Always-cool,
When spring-storms sound
In the greening hills.

2
So quiet are the green forests
Of our homeland,
The crystalline wave
Dying on a ruined wall
& we wept in sleep;
Along the thorny hedge,
In the summer evening,
Singers wandered
With hesitant steps in the holy peace
Of the distant vineyard;
Shadows now in the cool lap
Of night, sorrowing eagles.
So quietly a moonbeam closes
The crimson wounds of melancholy.

3
You mighty cities
Built from stone
On the plain!
Speechless the homeless one
Follows the wind
With dark brow,
The bare trees on the hill.
You distant fading streams!
The hideous red sunset
Breeds fear
In the thunderclouds.
You dying peoples!
Pale wave
Breaking on the beach of night,
Stars that are falling.

Springtime of the Soul

A sudden cry in sleep; the wind plunges through black alleys,
The blue of spring beckons through breaking branches,
The night-dew is purple & all around the stars go out.
The river is green in the dusk, the old avenues silver
& the towers of the city. O gentle drunkenness
In the gliding boat & the dark calls of the blackbird
In childlike gardens. Already, the rosy veil thins & lifts.

The solemn rush of water. Moist shadows of the floodplain,
The border animal; green shapes, flowering branches
Touch the crystal forehead; shimmering swaying boat.
Softly the sun sings through rose-colored clouds by the hill.
Great is the stillness of the fir forest, the serious shadows at the
    river.

Purity! Purity! Where are the terrible paths of death,
Of grey stony silence, the rocks of the night
& the restless shadows? Radiant the abyss of the sun.

Sister, when I found you at the lonely clearing
Of the forest, & it was noon & the great silence of animals;
Whiteness under wild oak, & the thorn blossomed silver.
Enormous dying & the singing flame in the heart.

The waters flow more darkly around the beautiful play of fishes.
Hour of grief, silent vision of the sun;
The soul is a strange shape on earth. Blueness lingers
In spirit over the pruned forest; & a dark bell tolls
Long in the village; peaceful attendance.
Silently the myrtle blooms above the white eyelids of the dead one.

Quietly the waters sound at the end of the afternoon
& the wilderness grows darker on the green shore; there is joy in the rosy wind;
The brother's soft song by the evening hill.

In Darkness

The soul silences the blue springtime.
Under moist evening branches
The brows of the lovers shuddered & sank.

O Cross of greenness. In the dark
The man & the woman knew each other.
At the bare wall
The solitary man walks on with his stars.

Over the moonlit paths of the forest
Forgotten huts
Sank in the wilderness; a blue gaze
Breaks from decayed rocks.

Song of the Departed

To Karl Borromaeus Heinrich

The flight of birds is full of harmonies. The green forests
Gather in the evening to more silent cabins;
The crystal meadows of the deer.
A dark shape calms the brook, the moist shadows,

& the flowers of summer that ring so beautifully in the wind.
Already the brow of the pondering man grows gloomy & dark.

& a small lamp shines, the goodness in his heart
& the peace of the meal; because holy is the bread & wine
From the hands of God, & from eyes of night & silence
The brother gazes at you, & rests from thorny wanderings.
O to dwell in the soulful blueness of the night.

Lovingly the silence in the room also embraces the shades of
 ancestors,
The scarlet torments, laments of a great generation,
Passed on & fading with the lonely grandchild.

Because the sufferer wakes radiant from black minutes of madness
Enduring at the stony threshold
& is embraced by the cool forceful blueness & the bright end of
 autumn,

The silent house & the legends of the forest,
Measure & law & the moonlit paths of the departed.

Section 5: Dream & Derangement

Dream & Derangement

1.

In the evening the father became an old man; in dark rooms the face of the mother turned to stone & the curse of the degenerate family weighed on the boy. Sometimes he remembered his childhood, filled with sickness, terror, and darkness, secretive games in the star-garden, or that he fed the rats in the darkening courtyard. From the blue mirror stepped the slender form of his sister & he fell as though dead into darkness. At night his mouth burst open like a red fruit & stars shone over his speechless grief. His dreams filled the ancient house of his fathers. In the evening he liked to walk over the ruined cemetery, or he watched the corpses in the darkening crypts, the green stains of decay on their beautiful hands. At the gate of the monastery he asked for a piece of bread; the shadow of a black horse jumped out of darkness & frightened him. When he lay in his cool bed, unspeakable tears overcame him. But there was no one who might have put a hand on his forehead. When autumn came, he walked, a clairvoyant, in brown meadow. O, the hours of wild ecstasy, the evenings by the green river, the hunting. O, the soul which quietly sang the song of the yellowed reed; fiery piety. Silently & long he looked into the star-eyes of the toad, felt with trembling hands the coolness of the old stone & discussed the venerable legend of the blue spring.   O, the silver fish & fruits which fell from stunted trees. The chords of his steps fulfilled him with pride & contempt of men. On the way home, he came upon an uninhabited palace. Gods in their ruin stood in the garden, mourning in the evening. But it seemed to him: here I lived forgotten years. An organ choral fulfilled him with God's awe. But he spent his days in a dark cave, lied & stole & hid, a flaming wolf before the white face of the mother. O, the hour when with a stony mouth he sank down in the star-garden, & the shadow of the murderer came over him. With a purple forehead he walked into the moor & God's wrath chastised his metal shoulders; o, the birches in the storm, the dark animals which avoided his deranged paths. Hate burned his heart, lust, when in the green summer garden he violated the silent child & recognized his own mad face in the child's radiating one. Woe, in the evening at the window, when the grayish skeleton of death stepped out of purple flowers. O, you towers & bells; & the shadows of night fell like stone upon him.

2.

No one loved him. His head burned away falsehood & immorality in darkening rooms. The blue rustle of a woman's dress stiffened him into a column & in the doorway stood the nocturnal figure of his mother. Above his head the shadow of evil rose up. O nights & stars. In the evening he walked up the mountain with the cripple; the rosy splendor of sunset lay on the icy peak & his heart rang softly in the twilight. The stormy firs sank heavily upon them & the red hunter stepped out of the forest. When night came his heart broke crystal-like & darkness beat his forehead. Under bare oak trees he strangled a wild cat with icy hands. The white figure of an angel appeared lamenting to his right, & the shadow of the cripple grew larger in the dark. But he lifted a rock & threw it at the other so that he fled howling & in the shadow of the tree the gentle face of the angel vanished sighing. He lay a long time on a stony acre gazing with astonishment at the golden tent of the stars. Chased by bats, he rushed into the darkness. Breathless, he entered the decayed house. In the courtyard he drank the well's blue water like a wild animal until he became cold. Feverish, he sat upon the icy stairs, raging against God, that he might die. O, the grey face of terror when he raised his round eyes over a dove's slit throat. Slipping away over strange stairs, he met a whore & he grabbed her black hair & seized her mouth. Hostile shapes followed him through dark streets & an iron clattering tore his ear. Along autumnal walls like an altar boy he silently followed the silent priest; drunkenly he breathed in the scarlet of his sacred cassock under the withered trees. O, the ruined disk of the sun. Sweet torments consumed his flesh. In a deserted passageway his own bleeding form appeared to him bristling with filth. He loved the sublime works of stone more deeply; the tower that nightly storms the blue sky with hellish grimaces; the cool grave in which the fact of man's fiery heart is preserved. Woe to the unspeakable guilt testified to by the heart. But when he walked along the autumnal river under bare trees thinking intently on something blazing, his sister appeared to him as a flaming daemon in a hair shirt. As he woke, the stars expired above her head.

3.

O cursed family. When in polluted rooms the destiny of everyone has been fulfilled, death enters the house with rotting steps. O, that it was spring & a lovely bird was singing in the blossoming tree out there. But the scanty green withers to gray on the windows of the nocturnal ones & the bleeding hearts still ponder evil. O dark spring paths of the contemplative. More righteously he rejoices in the blossoming hedge, the farmer's young crop, & the singing bird, God's gentle creature; the evening bell & the beautiful community of men. So that he might forget his fate & the thorny sting. Freely the brook grows green, where his foot wanders silver-like, & a telling tree rustles above his deranged head. Thus he lifts the snake with lank hand & in fiery tears his heart melted away. The silence of the forest is sublime, darkness grown green, & mossy animals fluttering upward when night comes. O the terror when every being knows its guilt, walks thorny paths. Thus he found the white figure of the child in the thorn-bush bleeding for the coat of its bridegroom. But he stood mute & suffering before her, buried in his steel-like hair. O the radiant angels, whom the purple night wind dispersed. All night he dwelled in a crystalline cave & leprosy grew silver-like on his forehead. A shadow, he walked down the mule track under autumn stars. Snow fell, & blue darkness filled the house. The harsh voice of the father called out like a blind man & evoked dread. Woe of the bowed appearance of women. Under stiffened hands the terrified family's good & household goods crumbled into ruin. A wolf tore apart the firstborn & the sisters fled into dark gardens to bony old men. Deranged seer, he sang along the ruined walls & God's wind swallowed his voice. O lust of death. O children of a dark race. Silver-like the evil flowers of the blood glimmer on his temple, the cold moon in his broken eyes. O those of the night, O cursed ones.

4.

Deep is the slumber in dark poisons, filled with stars & the white stony face of the mother. Bitter is death, the fare of the guilt-laden; in the brown branches of the family tree the earthen faces disintegrated grinning. But quietly he sang in the green shadow of the elderberry, when he woke from bad dreams; a rosy angel approached him like a sweet playmate, so that he slumbered into the night like a gentle animal; & he saw the star-countenance of purity. The sunflowers sank golden over the garden fence when the summer came. O the diligence of bees & the green leaves of the walnut tree; the thunderstorms passing by. The poppy also bloomed silver-like, & bore our nocturnal star-dreams in green bud. O, how silent the house was when the father departed into the darkness. The fruit ripened purple on the tree & the gardener busied his hard hands; o the sackcloth-like signs in the radiant sun. But silently in the evening the shadow of the dead man entered the grieving family circle & his step sounded crystalline over the green meadow before the forest. The silent ones gathered around the table; dying ones with waxen hands they broke the bread that bleeds. Woe for the sister's stony eyes, when at the meal her insanity moved also onto the brother's forehead, when the bread of the mother turned to stone under suffering hands. O for the rotted ones, when with silver tongues they held their silence about hell. Thus the lamps in the cool room died out & through purple masks the suffering humans looked at each other silently. The rain poured down all night, & revived the meadow. In thorny wilderness the dark one followed the yellowed paths in the grain, following the song of the lark & the gentle stillness of green branches, so that he might find peace. O, you villages & mossy steps, glowing sight. But bonily the steps stagger over sleeping snakes at the forest edge & the ear follows the raving scream of the vulture. In the evening he found a stony solitude, a dead man's to escort him into the dark house of the father.

5.

A purple cloud covered his head, so that he silently attacked his own blood & effigy, a moon-like face; he sank stonily away into emptiness, when the dying youth his sister appeared in a broken mirror; the night swallowed the cursed family.

IV

Published in *Der Brenner* 1914-5

In Hellbrun

Following again the evening's blue cry,
Along the hill, the spring pond—
As if shadows of those-long dead, shadows
Of prelates & exalted ladies, hovered above --
Already their flowers bloom, the grave violets
In the hollows of evening, already the crystal wave
Of the blue spring ripples there. They blossom & are holy,
The oaks above the forgotten paths of the dead,
The gold cloud over the pond.

The Heart

The wild heart turned white at the wood's edge.
O dark fear
Of death, that the gold
Died in a gray cloud.
November evening.
A group of poor women
Standing at the bare door of the slaughter house.
Into every basket
The spoiled meat, the entrails;
O cursed food!

The blue dove of evening
Brought no reconciliation.
The dark blare of the trumpets
Pierced through the leaves,
Wet & gold, of the elms,
A torn flag
Steaming with blood,
So that the man listens carefully
In a wild sadness.
O bronze ages
Buried there in sunset.

From the dark hallway
A young girl stepped out,
A gold shape
Surrounded by pale moons,
The autumn entourage,
That broke black pines
In the night-storm
& the steep fortress.

O heart
Shining into the snowy cold.

Sleep

To hell with your dark poisons,
White sleep!
This strangest of gardens,
Twilight trees
Filled with snakes, night-moths,
Spiders, bats.
Stranger, it is your lost shadow
At sunset,
A dark pirate ship
On the salt-ocean of sorrow.
White birds fly up along night's edge
Over falling cities
Of steel.

Storm

You wild mountains, noble
Grief of eagles.
Gold clouds
Smoke above the stony waste.
The pines breath patient stillness,
& the black lambs on the abyss,
Where the blue suddenly
Grows strangely mute,
The soft hum of bees.
O green flower—
O Silence!

Dark & dreamlike, spirits of the torrent
Terrify the heart.
Darkness
That breaks in upon the gorges!
White voices
Straying through terrible vestibules.
Terraces torn apart,
Immense & violent anger of fathers,
Sad cries of mothers,
The boy's gold battle-cry,
& the unborn
Groaning with blind eyes.

O grief, fiery vision
Of immense spirits!
Already in the black tumult
Of horses & carriages,
The rose-terrible bolt of lightning
Flashes in the ringing spruce.

Magnetic cool
Hovers around this proud head,
The burning sorrow
Of an angry God.

Fear, venomous snake,
Black one, die in stone!
Now wild streams
Of tears run down,
Storm-pity,
Echoing in menacing thunder
Around the snowy peaks.
Fire
Purifies the torn night.

Evening

Moon, you fill
The silent forest with
The dead shapes of heroes,
Crescent moon—
With the soft embrace
Of Lovers,
Shadows of the great ages
Around the decaying rock;
The light shines bluish
Toward the city
Where cold & wicked
A decaying race
Prepares a dark future
For the white grandsons.
Their moon-twisted shadows
Sigh in the empty crystal
Of a mountain lake.

Night

I sing you, wild cliffs,
Towering mountains,
In the night-storm;
You gray towers
Overflowing with faces of hell,
Fiery beasts,
Rough ferns, pines,
Crystal flowers,
Eternal torment,
You sought God
Gentle spirit,
Groaning in the cataract,
In the swaying pines.

The fires of nations
Burn gold everywhere.
Drunk with death
The whirlwind of light
Plunges over black cliffs,
The blue wave
Of the glacier
& the bell
Thunders in the valley:
Flames, curses,
& the dark
Games of lust,
A petrified head
Storms the heavens.

Sadness

Dark moon
Immense, inward
Shaped by autumn clouds,
& the stillness of gold evenings;
A green mountain stream in twilight,
Shadow zone
Of shattered pines;
A village
Devoutly fading in brown sepia prints.

See the black horses run
In the misty pasture.
Soldiers!
Laughing blood pours
From the hill where the sun rolls dying....
Under the silent
Oaks!
O bitter sadness
Of the army; a shining helmet
Sank clattering from a purple brow.

Autumn night comes
Cool, shining with stars,
Like a silent nun
Above the shattered remains.

Homecoming

The coolness of dark years,
Pain & Hope
Preserved by cyclopean rock,
Abandoned mountains,
Autumn's gold breath,
Evening cloud—
Purity!

Crystal childhood
Looks on with blue eyes;
Under dark spruce
Love, Hope,
Dew that falls
From fiery eyelids onto the stiff grass—
Incessantly!

There:—
The gold path
Breaks in the snow
Of the abyss!
The dark valley
Breathes blue coolness,
Faith, Hope!
Lonely churchyard, welcome!

Lament

Child, your gold gaze sank
From your crystal mouth into the valley;
The woods trembling red & lifeless
Wave in the black evening hour.
Evening strikes such deep wounds!

Fear! The dream-sickness of death,
The withered grave & the spent
Year gazes from the tree & deer;
A sallow field, & an acre of land.
The shepherd calls the frightened sheep.

Your blue brows, sister,
Beckons gently in the night.
The organ groans & hell laughs
& the heart is seized with horror—
It would like to look upon star & angel.

The mother must fear for her child;
The ore sounds suddenly red in the pit,
Lust, tears, stony sorrow,
The dark legends of the Titans,
Sadness! Sad cries of solitary eagles.

Night Surrender

Holy Sister, let your darkness embrace me,
Your mountains so cold & blue!
The dew bleeds down & is dark;
The cross looms up against the glittering stars.

When the mouth & the lie finally broke
There was purple in the room's decaying coolness;
Then the laughter shone, then the gold game,
Then the last windings of the clock.

A cloud across the moon! At night,
Wild fruit falls black from the tree,
& the room becomes a grave,
& this earthly pilgrimage a dream.

In The East

The grim anger of nations,
Like the wild organ-sounds of the winter storm,
The purple wave of battle,
Stars that have shed their leaves.

With shattered foreheads & silver arms
Night calls to the dying soldiers.
The spirits of the battle-dead groan
In the shadows of autumnal ash.

A desert of thorns surrounds the city.
The moon chases the terrified women
From steps that are bleeding.
Wild wolves have broken through the gate.

Klage

Those grave eagles, Sleep & death,
Cry all night about this head:
Man's gold image
Could disappear under
The icy wave of eternity. The purple body
Breaks on fearful reefs
& a dark voice cries
Over the sea.
Sister of the stormy sorrow
Look, the terrified boat sinks
Under stars
& the silent face of night.

Grodek

Evening & the killing weapons sound
In the autumn woods, the gold plains
& blue lakes, where the sun
Rolls dark & menacing; the night holds
Dying soldiers to itself, the wild
Cries of their shattered mouths.
Yet quietly in the low pasture there gather
Red clouds in which an angry god lives,
The spilt blood, the moonlike coolness;
All roads lead to black decay.
Under gold branches of the night & stars
The sister's shadow moves trembling through the silent grove
To greet the spirits of the heroes, their heads bleeding;
& the dark flutes of autumn sound softly from the reeds.
O prouder grief! You bronze altars
The hot flame of the spirit is fed today by an immense pain,
The unborn grandsons.

Revelation & Decline

1.

The dark paths of men are strange. When I was sleepwalking I passed rooms of stone & in each there burned a small motionless lamp, a copper candlestick, & when I collapsed freezing on my bed at its head the black shadow of the strange woman stood there again, & slowly & silently I buried my face in my hands. The hyacinth at the window had also blossomed into blue, & the old prayer came to Odmenden's purple lips, the world-bitterness bringing crystal tears. In this hour of the death of my father I was the white son. The night-wind shivered, from the hill in blue rain, & with it the dark cry of the mother was fading again, & I saw the black hell in my own heart —that moment of glittering quiet. Softly, a face that I cannot describe emerged from the chalky wall—it was a dying youth, the beauty of a race returning home. Moon-white, the coolness of stone embraces the waking temple, the footsteps of shadows fade on the ruined stairs, & the dance among the roses in the little garden.

2.

I sat silent & alone, drinking wine in the abandoned inn under charred wooden beams; a shining corpse bent over the dark one & a dead lamb lay at my feet. The pale figure of the sister emerged then from the decayed blue, her mouth bleeding, saying: Black thorn, pierce. Alas, still I hear the ringing of silver arms from the fierce storms. Blood, flow from the lunar feet that bloom on dark paths the shrieking rat flits past. Stars flare in my arched eyebrows, & gently the heart sounds in the night. A red shadow with a burning sword broke into the house, then fled with a brow of snow. O bitter death.

Then a dark voice spoke from within me: I broke the neck of my black horse in the night-forest, because there was madness in his purple eyes; the shadows of elms fell on me, the blue laughter of the fountain

& the black coolness of the night, & I was a wild hunter pursuing the snow-white deer; my face died away in a hell of stone.
Then a glittering drop of blood fell in the wine of the Lonely One; & as I drank it, it was more bitter than the poppy; & a black cloud enveloped my head, the crystal tears of the drowned angels; & gently the blood ran from the sister's silver wounds & a fiery rain fell on me.

3.

I want to be a silent thing walking at the wood's edge, one from whose mute hands the sun of hair descends; a stranger at the hill of night who weeps & opens his eyes over the city of stone; a deer standing motionless in the peace of the ancient elder; o the brain filled by twilight casts about, listening restlessly, or the hesitant footsteps follow the blue cloud on the hill, & the grave constellations. Nearby, the green corn goes along silently, & the timid young deer comes with us on the mossy wood-paths. The huts in the villages are closed up & silent & the blue lament of their mountain torrent is frightening in the black calm of the wind.

But as I climbed down the cliff-path, madness seized me & I cried out into the night; & as I bent with silver fingers over the silent water, I saw myself faceless. And the white voice spoke to me: Kill yourself! The shadow of the child groaned & rose up in me & saw me radiant with his crystal eyes, so that I fell weeping under the trees, the enormous vault of the stars.

4.

The restless journey through the wild rock so far from the towns of evening, & the birds returning home; far away the sun lowers itself & grazes in the crystal pasture, its wild song shaking us like something violent, the bird's lonely cry died in the blue calm. But you come softly in the night as I lay still awake on the hill or when madness has taken me in the spring thunder-storm; the sad clouds darken above the head of the dead one, horrible flashes of lightning terrify the dark spirit, your hands tear to pieces my breast from which all breath is gone.

5.

As I entered the twilight garden & the black form of evil had abandoned me, the hyacinth calm of night embraced me; & I sailed in my arched boat over the calm water, & a sweet calm touched my petrified brow. I lay dumb under the old willows & the blue sky above me was high & filled with stars; my thinking self died away & fear & sorrow died their heavy deaths in me; the blue shadow of the boy rose up shining in the darkness, singing softly; it rose then, on moon-like wings above the crystal reefs, the white face of the sister.

6.

I climbed down the thorny steps with silver soles & entered the whitewashed chamber. The candlestick burned quietly within & I buried my head silently in purple linen. The earth threw out a child-like corpse, a creation of the moon, that slowly stepped from my shadow, & the lid of stone sank down on smashed arms, flakes of snow.

About the Translator

Bob Herz is editor and publisher of *Nine Mile Magazine,* Nine Mile Books, the Nine Mile Talk About Poetry blog and the Talk About Poetry podcasts which appear on SoundCloud and iTunes. He is a graduate of the University of Iowa Writer's Workshop. He lives and works in Syracuse, NY.